The Prime Time

. . . and other writings

The Prime Time

. . . and Other Writings

By

Garland O. Goodwin

With two columns by his wife
Frances H. Goodwin

2009

Book contains
60 columns from *Prime Times!*
Plus
Some Piano and Airplane stories

Copyright ©2009 by Garland O. Goodwin
All rights reserved

ISBN # 1-4392-6583-6

Printed by
BookSurge Publishing
7290B Investment Drive
North Charleston SC 29412

Most of these essays first appeared in *Prime Times!* published in Henderson County NC between 2001 and 2005, whose rights in them has expired.

Other books by Garland O. Goodwin:
A Boy in the Amen Corner ©1999
Fat Fenders and Reflections ©2008

Printed in the United States of America

For Elaine Mueller, Anne Smith and the late Madalyn Green

TABLE OF CONTENTS

Preface -- xi
***Prime Times!* Columns:**
Christmas in the Thirties ---------------------------- 1
A Piece of Cake -- 3
Romance for Jean -------------------------------------- 8
Everybody Else Talks Funny---------------------- 11
They Cook Funny, Too ------------------------------ 13
Senior Citizen Joys ---------------------------------- 16
Our Dumb Animal Friends------------------------ 19
Technology: Servant or Master? ---------------- 21
Home Décor-- 24
Christmas in the Thirties II ------------------------ 26
The Prime Time -------------------------------------- 29
Ah, Romance!-- 32
Dance -- 35
Our Environment------------------------------------ 40
Turbo, the Supercharged Cat -------------------- 39
Ancestors -- 43
School Days in the 30s and 40s ------------------ 45
Wilbur was Right! ---------------------------------- 48
Wildlife -- 51
One Man's Toys-------------------------------------- 55
Toys Men Especially Love ------------------------ 58
Toys for Women ------------------------------------ 60
The Folly of Prophecy------------------------------ 63
Money!-- 65

Some Questions	68
Winter: BAH-AH!	71
Mother	74
My Dad, My Hero	77
Party Animal	80
The Weekend	83
For Love of Books	86
Ants & Grasshoppers	89
Food and Recipes	91
Gifts from the Heart	94
The Flexible Retiree	97
What's Good for the Heart	100
Computer for Fun & Profit	103
A Place in the Yard	107
Home Interiors Primer for Men	110
Ode to Our Personal Services People	112
The Veteran	116
Groceries in My Lifetime	120
How to Save Money	124
Getting There	128
A Traditional Christmas	131
Santa Claus	134
Self Improvement	136
Hobbies and Sports	138
New Food Favorites	142
Home and Garden	144
Summer Fun	147
Antique Collectibles	150
Sharing Vacation Memories	153

The Apples of My Eye ---------------------------- 158
A Life-Changing Moment ----------------------- 162
Wartime Memories -------------------------------- 165
An Incredible Gift --------------------------------- 169
The Communication of Love--------------------- 172
February is the Month for Lovers -------------- 173

Piano stories:
Mason & Hamlin Story --------------------------- 175
A Steinway Among Steinways ------------------ 177
Name Dropper ------------------------------------- 180

Airplane stories:
Young Texan Meets General Lindbergh ------ 192
A Gift of Wings ------------------------------------ 193
For Love of Airplanes ----------------------------- 196
Pilot in Command --------------------------------- 214

Preface

This book contains the sixty columns I wrote for *Prime Times!* between December 2001 and 2006 and some other writing my wife Fran and I have done.

Prime Times! was a monthly magazine published by Town Publishing of Hendersonville for senior citizens and distributed free in several counties of Western North Carolina, its production cost paid by its advertising revenues. Editor Madalyn Green invited me to write for her after Jacquie Ziller, formerly of the Travel and Tourism Office in Tryon, gave her my name.

Several months passed before I sent her copies of some of my *Bulletin* columns and asked if they were the sort of thing she wanted. We agreed on some slightly reworked columns and they began to appear in *Prime Times!* I met the other writers at Madalyn's Christmas party and enjoyed socializing with my newfound friends.

Then Madalyn was stricken with a terminal illness and we lost a great friend. But as in show business, life must go on, and our new editor, Anne Smith, continued to make writing fun and even began to send checks for our columns!

Publisher Elaine Mueller continued to host parties for the staff and to encourage us with ideas for making *Prime Times!* more attractive to more people. Then Elaine suffered a stroke that frightened her into selling the business. The new owner immediately began to liquidate its assets, and eventually closed the office, thus ending the life of *Prime Times!*

I used to do my part to increase circulation by handing out some two hundred copies each month. No one ever refused them, and many said they looked forward to getting them. Some even began to pick them up themselves on the newsstands! My mother-in-law commented that *Prime Times!* was the best newspaper she saw, because the words were used correctly and spelled right!

Town Publishing's rights in my columns expired some years ago, so I do not need permission to reprint them here. I am still in touch with some of the writers and staff of what to us was a great little family enterprise. The columns re-published herein are widely varied in scope and subject matter, written more to entertain than to inform. If you do happen to learn something, I hope you will still be smiling from whatever came before.

Like my previous books, this one takes its title from one of the columns inside: "The Prime Time" may be found on page 29.

Included is a column Fran contributed to *Prime Times!* (p.173) and another she sent to the *Tryon Daily Bulletin* (p.192) for its celebrity encounters series. There are some piano stories I wrote for my piano enthusiast friends, both players and technicians, followed by some articles about airplanes.

Christmas in the Thirties
December 2000

  Christmas has been a major happening in my life as long as I can remember. When I was a child in the 30s we went from having a very good income to having almost none. Of course I did not know why we moved so often and lived near or with so many different relatives in the span of a few years. But whatever the rest of the year had held, Christmas brought everyone together for a family celebration.
  My father would take us out into the woods to find a cedar tree to decorate. The cedar had a special aroma that followed it into the house and lingered with it; I still associate that aroma with Christmas and happiness. We had electric lights for our tree, and store-bought garlands and lead foil "icicles," but many farms did not have electricity then and the tree was often festooned with handmade decorations. Bright colored berries were strung or beautiful hand-dyed yarns were woven into garlands. The children made garlands as long chains by pasting the ends of colored paper strips together to make the links.
  Bowls of nuts and hard candy appeared around the house; we had to crack the shells off the black walnuts and the hard-shell pecans with a hammer and carefully pick out the edible part. We really

savored those little treats that we worked so hard to get at! I think our mothers consciously controlled our intake by the tedious removal of the nut meats and the long melting time of the hard candies; is that possible?

The kitchen was warmed by the cook stove and another room by a wood burning heater or fireplace; the rest of the house was nearly as cold as the outside. A brick warmed by the fire would be wrapped in flannel to be taken to bed with us to warm our feet and bring on the sandman. The last thing we did was to hang a long sock (preferably one of Daddy's) on the mantel for Santa to fill.

There were always goodies under the tree and in our stockings. The lumps in the sock were mostly apples and oranges, maybe tangerines, but there might be an onion to indicate that any substandard behavior on our part had been noticed. There was always at least one new toy, and in the good years perhaps something that was big enough to ride.

The best part was gathering at Grandma's house for the big Christmas tree and a big dinner. All the aunts and uncles and cousins by the dozens would be there. All the big people would always comment on how much we little people had grown, but the loving pat on the head by an uncle might be accompanied by a quarter tip!

Everything on the table got there by the sweat of someone's brow: it was all grown and made ready right there on the farm. Last year's hog was represented by a ham; the cow by fresh milk, buttermilk and a big bowl of butter; the chicken house by some younger fryers instead of the usual senior hen; the basement by vegetables put up in Mason jars last summer; and the kitchen by cornbread, biscuits, pies and cakes lovingly prepared by the women folk present. It was truly a feast fit for a king, so most of the afternoon was devoted to its enjoyment in shifts at the big dining table and several smaller tables brought in for the children.

I have celebrated many Christmases over the years, some all by myself on a far away Air Force base, some with only my wife and far from our families, but most with as many family members and friends as could be gathered. As the emphasis shifted from self to others and from Santa to Christ, Christmas became more meaningful. The details change, but Christmas is still a major happening for me. I hope it is for you, too. Merry Christmas!

A Piece of Cake
January 2001

If we live long enough we will get new eyes, new hips, new knees, etc. It is starting to come true for me: I have two new teeth courtesy of my dentist (he calls them crowns.) I have also participated in another miracle of modern medicine: Dr. Thomas Perraut removed the cataract-laced lens from my right eye, and inserted a new man-made lens that is as clear as nothing and focuses on the retina of my misshapen eyeball.

Everyone who learned that I was to get a new lens said that the operation is a "piece of cake." Everyone. The same words to describe the experience. I now believe that description is pretty apt from the patient's point of view, but I daresay the surgeon might not regard it so lightly. I am profoundly grateful that Dr. Perraut learned how to do the procedure and was willing to do it for me.

Both he and Dawn McCullough smiled a lot, but in dealing with me, they had their work cut out for them. They have the patience of Job and I that of a yellow jacket (for you Yankees, that is a very aggressive sort of bee found Down Here.)

Dr. Thomas Perraut

Dawn would go over and over that chart with me, trying to get me to assign a letter or a number to those fuzzy little blobs thereon. Then it was "look at the red light and open WIDE," a hundred times for each eye. With my fat head come fat eyelids, and they just don't open very wide. So she would reach across the machine, have me look down to uncover enough lid to pull up, and then hold it while she manipulated the machine with the other hand. "Look down, now look straight ahead . . . red light . . . "

Immediately after the surgery, I went to tour the [Polk County] Courthouse with the other members of the Restoration committee. I had a mask over the operated eye, and I walked through all the dust and commotion of two dozen workmen doing their thing, without a thought that my action might be inadvisable. Next morning Dr. Perraut discovered an abrasion on my cornea, and installed a contact lens to cover and protect it while it healed. He was grinning as he remarked that he could not sit on me, but would I please listen again to the precautions, remember them, and don't . . .

Well, I soon brushed a small piece of plastic off my cheek. A while later, it occurred to me that it might have been that contact lens. Back to the office, where Dr. Perraut put in another lens that fit better and did not fall out. Since then it has been drops and more drops, but I have stopped taping a protective mask over the eye, and instead wear my glasses with one window out. I have been greeting people by poking a finger through the frame where there is no lens to show that I am seeing them with a very naked eye.

The first thing I noticed with my new lens was that what I saw was brighter and colors more vivid. The old left eye still saw everything through a yellow filter. Do you remember from your Crayola days that blue and yellow make green? Then I saw that my shirt has blue stripes with my right eye and green stripes with my left eye.

When I was growing up, no girls wore glasses and the only boys who did were the ones who desperately needed them. When the doctor put my first pair on me, and then tried to take them back to adjust them, I grabbed them and held on tight. He had to pry my hands loose while assuring me that I would get to keep them. I was nine years old.

The distortion of distance and direction produced by my lenses meant that I could not track a baseball well enough either to catch it or to hit it. My glasses also ruled out contact sports, so I was pretty much left out of the normal boy's world. I could run well and climb the mountain like a goat, but who wants to play with a goat?

Our life is pretty much what we make it, but having to wear glasses is more limiting than people who enjoy good vision without them can imagine. You cannot wipe your brow on your sleeve, and the sweat runs onto the lenses so that you cannot see what you are trying to do. Rain does the same thing.

The swimming pool is a problem because you cannot tell who the other people are, and diving is fraught with other dangers. The plastic frames fit so tight against the nose and cheeks that no air circulates behind the lenses. If you move your head, the whole world shifts, and you have to let things settle into place before you reach for anything. Vertical lines, like the sides of buildings, are curved. And if you take off your glasses, you cannot find them again unless you remember exactly where you put them.

On the positive side, glasses do protect your eyes somewhat. Dirt does not fall into them when you crawl under the car to adjust something. Since the eyes offer an immediate route into your bloodstream, the lenses offer valuable protection against drops of liquid sent your way by sneezes or something unsanitary you might be working on.

Now I am free from the tyranny of glasses! Dr. Perraut replaced my other cataract-infested lens, and I am seeing better than I ever saw in my life. Gone are the problems outlined above, and instead there is a clear, undistorted view of our beautiful world. Colors are bright and right. There is no blinding glare from bright lights at night. I find myself just looking at people and things to savor the clarity, color and detail. Straight lines are straight. Squares are square. Blue is blue and green is green.

The engineers are helping the doctors to give us replacement parts that are nearly as good as those we came with. Not only mechanical equivalents, but computer chips that mimic brain functions to allow people to hear, see, and walk. I consider myself fortunate to have lived through the good ol' days to these better new days.

When I told my Fran at supper the day after my first eye surgery that I could now see every little wrinkle in her face, even the blood vessels in her eyeballs, she just stared at me for a moment. Then she said, "I'm for telling the doctor to put that thing back!"

Romance for Jean?
February 2001

In the 1940s, my Uncle Pete supplemented the income from his farm by collecting milk from local farmers for the Biltmore Dairy near Asheville. The Biltmore herd of Jersey cows was one of the finest in the world. Whenever they changed to a new bloodline to maintain this supremacy, they would make heifers bred to the former bull available for purchase by their employees. My grandmother knew a good thing when she saw it, so she made a deal with Uncle Pete to obtain one of those heifers. Pete agreed to get one for her, if he could have the first heifer calf born.

Mama Rippy, as I called her, named her new heifer Jean. Jean soon dropped her first calf, Pete got his heifer, and Mama Rippy taught me how to milk Jean. I got a half-gallon of fresh milk per day for our family for milking Jean, plus all the buttermilk I wanted.

Things went along very well for a while. I made a pet of Jean, using the mule's currycomb to brush her coat. Some time later, Jean seemed to go wild. She began to bellow mightily, and was not in any way consoled by my attentions with the currycomb, did not care to be scratched under the chin or behind her ears. Since I was only eleven years old, I had no idea what had come over Jean.

Mama Rippy understood. She arranged with the owner a fine Jersey bull for me to bring Jean over. My destination could be seen from the hill above our house, but we had to go a quarter mile down our road and cross over a creek on a tiny wooden bridge to get to the highway. The highway wound through a village and crossed a river on a very narrow concrete bridge. We then had to take a dirt road about a half-mile to the barn where the bull lived.

I put a rope on Jean's horns and we started out. We went past the gate to her pasture, and started down the steep road to the highway. She bellowed with every other breath, but she kept going. Until we got to the little wooden bridge, that is. When her hooves began to clatter on the boards and she looked down through the cracks at the creek below, she stopped.

We had to get across that bridge. I finally persuaded her to follow me by holding her head up, and we then bawled our way through the village, causing all heads to turn. I had to wait until there were no cars coming either way to cross the concrete bridge, but we made it all right.

The bull's owner came out of his house at our approach (he probably had heard our progress since we left the highway) and opened the gate into the barnyard. He told me just to hold Jean right there and he went on into the barn. He soon reappeared, leading a large bull by a rope. The bull knew exactly what was expected of him, and he lost no time in performing the service. Jean and I were both mightily impressed by this proceeding; she became quiet, and the visual image is etched permanently into my brain cells.

Again all was well for a while, but not for long. Jean began to bellow again, and Mama Rippy told me that I had to take her back to the bull. This time, as we passed the gate to the pasture, the rope went taut as Jean went into a trot. We sailed over the wooden bridge, and right on through town. I really had a hard time getting her stopped until we could safely cross the concrete bridge, and we arrived at the other barn in record time. Jean had several more calves, but never another heifer.

I don't think much "romance" was involved in the above transaction, but I do know that many romantic encounters do lead to the sort of activity I witnessed. Happy Valentine's Day, and may Cupid find his mark unerringly!

Everybody Else Talks Funny
April 2001

As Tryon Little Theater's Professor Higgins railed once more about the "cold-blooded murder of the English tongue," I thought of the great variations in the way we Americans talk. Even before my Air Force years introduced me to accents from all over the country, I had noted differences right in my extended family.

An uncle in Durham spoke of planes dropping "bums" on Germany in WWII, and an aunt in lower South Carolina drank "wawtuh" when nothing more flavorful was at hand. I thought the clumps of tall grass I chopped down were broom "sage" until a few years ago, when I heard a new friend, whose business is stopping shoreline erosion, refer to various "sedges," which were similar in appearance to the stuff I dug up.

When a small boy I asked a new neighbor in Durham what kind of animal she was carrying, and reported to Mother that she had said it was a "dahg," but that it looked "sorta like a dawg" to me. It was a Pekinese. I have learned to say "fog" and "hog" as the neighbor lady did, but I still call man's best friend a "dawg."

How I say a word depends on where I learned it. I learned pretty good English at Mother's knee, but other words that I picked up just from hearing them represent quite a mixture. Californians commented that I did not have a Southern accent, but they were just being kind. They were not so kind to my new wife, Fran, when she arrived there from Texas. She went to work as a switchboard operator, and she talked with operators all over the country. She felt that people had no business making fun of her when they themselves had such weird speech habits.

Many Texans make no distinction between "card" and "cord," and she still has trouble with that sometimes. The collegians at Charlottesville VA hang out at a fine tavern called Lord Hardwicke's. Try though she might, it usually came out Lord Hordwicke, or else Lard Hardwicke. So whenever we drove through Charlottesville, I would suggest that we go to ol' Lard's place, but that is not funny to her.

At our local Red Cross blood drive, the refreshment lady asks me if I want "toe-MAH-toe" juice. I tell her she is lucky that I don't ask for "MAY-ter jewse," which might send even worse shivers up her spine than my "tuh-MAY-tuh." I asked another "come here" friend how he always knows it is I on the phone before I can say more than two words, and he claims not to know, for he says it could not be my "ACK-see-int."

Many of my dear friends here respond by saying "yay-iss," thus upholding our Southern tradition of making at least two syllables of words like "yes." And our habit of pronouncing each syllable separately in long words actually helps to distinguish one word from another: sometimes different words sound identical when the emphasis is properly placed: affect and effect, for instance.

And I think I have figured out why people from elsewhere think we sometimes say "y'all" to only one person: the "all" goes with the NEXT word, as in "Are y'all done with that? If y'are, I'd like to use it." The all done means completely finished with it, because if you are going to use it again right away, then "I'll wait til y'are all done with it." Makes sense to me.

They Cook Funny, Too!
May 2001

Three of my cousins invited me fly to Oshkosh with them to the big Air Show. We are all Southern boys, raised on proper Southern cooking. For one thing, that means that all vegetables are cooked thoroughly on top of the stove, with enough fatback thrown in to season them beyond recognition. Green beans just taste too "green" otherwise, but are delicious when properly cooked (see above) and served with raw sliced tomatoes and cucumbers. Hot cornbread with slabs of butter laid on, and buttermilk to fill in the hollow places in the stomach, complete a fine country meal.

We stayed in the nearby college dorm and took our morning and evening meals in its cafeteria. Breakfast offered many possibilities to satisfy any appetite (don't remember seeing any sorghum or grits, though), but supper was another matter. They generally offered beef, chicken or fish, but besides the potatoes and salads, there was only something called "mixed vegetables."

On the third night, as I watched cousin George struggling with yet another ton of steamed broccoli, I commented to him that people up there in Wisconsin not only talk funny, but they cook funny, too. He nodded with resignation as he continued to crunch on what to him should have been soft and easy.

It is not only regional cooking that is different. When a man marries, he discovers that his wife does not cook like his mom. Both might be great cooks, but there will be changes. My mother often catered to my whims when she should have told me to eat what she cooked and learn to like it.

During a visit, Mother came into the kitchen while wife Fran was cooking supper. She asked, "Will Garland be eating with us?" When assured that I would soon be home, she said, "Well, he would not have eaten any of this when he was growing up." That supper consisted entirely of my favorites!

My introduction to other cooking styles came slowly. I first tried pizza at a drive-in eatery in California, and decided immediately that it was "just chemicals." When we later had a class party at Bertolino's house, however, the pizzas, pastas and sauces were something else, and it then became difficult to find that level of good taste anywhere else.

To appreciate the difference between gourmet fare and fast food is one thing; to afford it is another. On a company trip, several of us were on inadequate *per diem*, while our leader was on unlimited expense account. A gourmet, he took us to fine restaurants where he ordered the wine and made dinner recommendations. I went along for the experience and the good company, but after a month of frequent fine dining, my wallet was pretty flat. At Nick's Seafood Pavilion in Yorktown VA, I ordered the cheapest dish I could find, spaghetti and meat sauce, I think. Our leader was utterly dismayed.

Some years later, I sometimes took Fran to Nick's to celebrate our wedding anniversary. I decided that it doesn't make much sense to order champagne when the Greek salad has a vinegar-based dressing. I would squeeze lemon juice into the drawn butter, then dunk my bite of lobster tail to enhance its delicate flavor. Better'n spaghetti!

So everybody else talks funny and eats funny. But I don't like pork chops any less from having discovered *filet mignon*. My veggies go down just fine whether raw, steamed, or well seasoned (except green beans). Even our friends from Up North are rejoicing that our Hardee's is serving grits again. I can deal with heavy or light *hors d'oevres* and fine wines and cheeses, but I still think that Toastchees washed down with Dr. Pepper are fine, too. I suppose the above explains why I am becoming such a well-rounded person as I enter my seventies. *Bon appetit,* y'all!

Senior Citizen Joys
August 2001

Most writing that I see for us Senior Citizens attempts to soften the consequences of getting older by making light of our maladies and things we can no longer do. While I usually grin and bear it, these essays have taught me that I am a most fortunate older person indeed.

My wife of some 46 years still lives with me and shows me in countless ways that she still loves me. Fran makes great pizza and peach cobbler and French Toast and scrambled eggs and it is a wonder that I am not more overweight than I am. She has her own computer to keep our social calendar and send warm greeting cards to our family and friends. I enjoy a magic house, for I just put my clothes in the hamper and they reappear on our bed neatly folded, or on hangers in my closet.

When we get in the car she tells me where to go, having compiled in her computer all the maps we will need and telling me about all the Air Museums I will want to see on the way. I used to pile everything and everybody in the car and roll out of our driveway before dawn, not stopping until the car needed something. I did allow for an evening meal in a restaurant before falling exhausted into the motel bed. Now we have a nice breakfast, drive to the first rest area, stop to smell the flowers when they present themselves, and quit driving well before dark in order to enjoy some of whatever our waypoint offers.

We are still in pretty good health. I have new eyes after cataract surgery, and Fran is about ready to get at least one new knee and maybe a new hip to increase her walking mileage. Her shopping cart serves her as a walker and she has no difficulty keeping it moving while filling it up. And what goes into the cart? Not just groceries and computer supplies; these empty-nesters are still putting in kid stuff!

What do I buy at the Gift Shops? Why, a Dr. Pepper bib and a Blue Angels tee shirt for a very special little person. Would she rather have Elmo or Barney? I never ask; if it is from her Pop-Pop, it is beautiful. Her mom can buy her shoes and the educational stuff. Granny buys her cute little dresses and hats. Leave the heavy-duty spoiling to the grandfolks, right?

Other joys of retirement are getting to read the most interesting-looking article in the new magazine as soon as it comes. Having time to read again books that you especially enjoyed or to pursue other simple pleasures that were forced off the agenda earlier in life. Having checks that are not wages deposited in your bank regularly. Shopping on weekday mornings so you can park up close and not wait in line when you get inside. Lunching quietly in restaurants after the noon rush. Hearing that "you sure don't look it," when you give your age for a senior discount. Finding that a long lost friend is still living, and would be glad to see you.

We recently took a long trip to see several such friends. The occasion was Fran's mother's 85th birthday celebration, attended by all of the family and a host of friends. En route we were treated like visiting royalty by people we had not seen for some 20 to 50 years. That's right, 50. I found him in an association directory that I bought just for that purpose. We had a lot of catching up to do, and he took us to a fine French restaurant to do it.

I join a former pastor in offering you Browning's
"Grow old along with me!
The best is yet to be . . ."

Our Dumb Animal Friends
September 2001

Why is it that animals that cannot speak to us in our language are considered less than smart? Science insists that animals make very limited use of language and tools, and that their emotions or feelings are pretty rudimentary as well. I read that when a dog or cat yawns, that merely means it is going to do something else now, and bears no relation to whether it is sleepy or bored. I think they yawn for the same reasons we do; why not?

We who have loved animals all of our lives are not surprised by the revelations about Koko, the gorilla who was taught sign language and began thus to communicate with her human "trainer." Koko has shown remarkable reasoning power and a wide emotional range much like ours. Experiments with an English-speaking bird showed it to have a good understanding of what it was saying and what was said to it.

Perhaps Dr. Doolittle could understand more of what the animals were telling him than most of us can, but our dogs and cats, horses and cows, even pigs, can tell us much without speaking English. I think the "horse whisperer" is on the right track. People who have never taken the time to build a relationship with an animal (or another person!) just don't know what they are missing!

My brother Bill acquired a golden retriever through a club that rescues these dogs and finds homes for them. Chelsea was everything one could want in a companion, so loving that you could not help loving her. Bill said he felt inadequate in showing her how much he loved her, and I agreed with him—how could we return that devotion that shone in her eyes and was evident in her every action toward us?

Bill was a prankster, and Chelsea seemed to understand and enjoy even that part of their relationship. He would give her a pill in peanut butter on a cracker, and when that was down, he would then give her another cracker with the peanut butter on top. He would laugh at her struggles with the stuff stuck on the roof of her mouth, but she would come right back for another. She did not mind being laughed at, since she got another cracker.

No cat will tolerate being laughed at. They are masters of all they survey, and when they goof they do not want it noticed. While most dogs are happy to be man's best friend right off, most cats require a little "courtship."

We have our son's cat because he can no longer keep her. Carrera is a beautiful Chartreuse and was the original "fraidy cat." She never said anything, and went under the bed to sleep after she ate. She was so aloof and afraid (big eyes, terrified look) that I decided to try to win her over.

I spoke to her gently and ran my hand down her back whenever she went by. She would flatten her ears and drop to a crouch so that I could barely touch her. After a while she would brush against my hand or leg in passing. If I found her sleeping in the open, I would stroke gently behind her ears while telling her softly how pretty she was. Nearly a year passed before she would come to me, curl up and go to sleep.

Now she is a neurotic old lady, who insists loudly that she wants to be fed NOW or that she wants to go outside NOW (that is not "meow" they are saying, just as no dog says "bow-wow"). But she closes her eyes slowly and purrs when she comes to me to have her fur brushed. It was worth it.

Technology: Servant or Master?
October 2001

The impact of technology on our lives is surely a mixed bag if there ever was one. The same is true of rain, food and fire, depending on how much of them we get. Since technology is a part of my school's name, and I spent 40 years of my life designing airplanes, I do know something about technology.

When asked what I think is the most important contribution to our lives made by the exploration of space, I usually review some of the obvious benefits: satellites (weather, TV, communication, mapping, positioning, etc.), integrated circuits (the "chips" in calculators, computers, TVs, cameras, hearing aids, etc.), lasers, Velcro, better materials and finishes, and so on. All of these things and much more came from the drive to put a man on the moon.

And what did the man discover on the moon? Rocks? Sure, but I think the most important thing he saw was that view of our beautiful blue and white earth rising above the barren moonscape. Why? Because it brought home to all of us the realization that our earth is a finite thing, a little ball hurtling through a very hostile space. Its gravity causes our life-sustaining atmosphere to cling to it. Everything we need to live is built into it, balanced and regulated within the narrow limits required for our survival. And if we mess it up, we don't have anywhere to go . . .

The people who settled America thought they had found an unlimited land of plenty. Even when viewed from the mountaintops it seemed to stretch on and on forever. With so much land available, there was no need to take care of it. The streams would clean themselves as they flowed over rocks and sand. The sky would absorb whatever was sent up into it and the wind would blow it away. The oceans were so huge that anything could be dumped into them without effect.

It is all still here, every bit of it. We have overwhelmed our planet's ability to clean and balance itself. We send Tennessee water they cannot drink, and they send us air we cannot breathe. Does that make us even? Everything we make is designed to be thrown away, not repaired or recycled. But where will we throw it?

I have found new owners for my cars and houses over the years, but what do I do with two printers that no longer work? What do I do with my big old stereo system, long-playing records and cassette tapes? When I go to tune pianos, I find electronic organs and keyboards that no longer work. Everyone has small appliances that no longer work. In most cases, they cannot be repaired, or a new one is better and costs less than any possible repairs. We personally recycle as much as we can, but an awful lot of stuff is still being buried somewhere . . . out of sight, out of mind, I suppose.

Of course I am thankful for air conditioning, indoor plumbing, wash-and-wear clothes, cars and airplanes, my computer, and my new lens implants that replaced my own cataract-laced lenses and allow me to see well without glasses for the first time in more than 60 years. Many of us live better and longer lives because of the blessings of technology, but overall we have not managed technology well: I think every so-called advance should provide for its own harmless assimilation back into the earth's storehouse.

Perhaps that photograph of the earth from the moon should be hung in every school and factory and home in the world to remind us that we are indeed all in the same boat. Would we then take better care of it?

Home Décor
November 2001

I usually write about things that I know about, such as last month's Technology column. This month it is Home Décor, and I have decided to take a stab at it. While I know very little about it, I do have some experience with it. Our daughter is a graduate of ECU's Interior Design program, and woe be unto anyone who refers to her as an "Interior Decorator!" Her degree qualifies her to modify the structure of the house if need be, but she can usually find a less drastic way to make your house work for you.

When she is hired to apply her talents to a builder's house to enhance its sales appeal, she can let her creative juices flow freely. She has numerous awards to show that people like what she does. But if you ask her to help with your house that you are going to live in, she will learn what your likes, tastes and needs are before she suggests anything.

When it was time to paint the dream house I designed and built for Fran and me to grow old in, of course I consulted Sharon. We had selected the colors for the siding and trim; they were fine. We wanted a neutral color scheme for the interior so that we could add such highlights as we wished later. When she sent us the color swatches, we liked them very much.

Fran wanted to paint the wall behind the head of our bed Hunter Green and add plastic lattice as trim and texture. Fine, but Sharon suggested painting ALL the walls of the bedroom Hunter Green. We did, and it looks great. Then she told me to paint the wall behind the built-in shelves in the den Hunter Green also. Never would have occurred to me, but the effect is beautiful and dramatic. She also said not to fill the shelves completely with books, but to leave spaces for small objects to be displayed. So we have grouped books by subject or type, and added all those little vases and other pretties that we have gathered over the years because we like them. So far, so good.

Then ol' Dad starts to hang the pictures. I know to confine my certificates and big airplane posters to my office, and the buxom Miss Makita to the workshop. Sharon told me that only art, not anything with words on it, could go in the formal rooms. She asked me whether the group that has been on the wall nearest the front door in every house all of her life would be going there in this house, too. Uh-oh.

The grouping consists of the Declaration of Independence and the Bill of Rights, with a portrait of Thomas Jefferson and a drawing of a Continental Soldier. Together they make a pretty good statement of who we are, and who we wanted our kids to be. It worked, and I still like for our visitors to get the same message right away. I think they are especially appropriate today.

Then there is the matter of the framed chronology of the composers of great music that relates them to their times. It was bequeathed to me by my piano teacher because I used to study it while waiting for my lesson. It hangs behind the piano bench. I got away with that, too, because it is not really noticeable unless you go over to play the piano.

An illustrated silkscreen version of the Psalm that begins "I will lift up mine eyes to the hills . . ." also hangs beside the big windows of the living room that offer us a wide view of our beautiful mountains. I think that is the perfect place for it; by then, Sharon just shrugged and moved on to the window treatments . . .

Sharon helped us with many ideas that make our house look better than it might have, and she has NOT asked us to tell people that she had nothing to do with it. Besides, she brings our granddaughter when she comes, and then no one notices anything else anyway!

Christmas in the Thirties II
December 2001

The first Christmas I can remember was celebrated in the mid thirties on Rippy Hill, the family name for my Grandfather Rippy's farm near

Lynn NC. I was four or five, and my brother Bill was too young to be involved. His days were pretty much the same, I guess—have his nap, have his bottle, bug his big brother some way, have another nap.

As we got older and I started to school, it was suggested that I write a letter to Santa. That was pretty effective, so it was easy for me to believe. Bill and I were on our best behavior for that fortnight—we did not start fights and annoy one another nearly so much. We were on the lookout for Santa on patrol—any moving light at night was a possibility—for we knew that he must be checking on us.

Daddy would take us out into the woods and cut a pretty cedar tree to be decorated. I shall always remember the prickly needles and the wonderful aroma that followed the tree into the house and lingered with it. We had electric lights and store-bought garlands left from a more affluent time, so our tree was pretty special. We hung the lead foil "icicles" with care so that they all hung straight down like the ones on the trees outside. The lights were molded in the shape of a pocket watch, a bird, a lantern, a bell, an angel, Santa and other things appropriate to the season. I have never seen any like them since, and we don't have them any more. Too bad.

During Christmas week bowls of nuts and hard candy appeared. The nuts had to be shelled by hammer and the meats carefully gouged out. We tacked our long socks to the mantel board before going to bed on Christmas Eve. Bricks heated by the fire were wrapped in flannel and taken to our cold bedroom to warm our feet and help send us off to dreamland.

In the morning there might be a store-bought toy under the tree, something we had earnestly wished for and confided to Santa. Our stocking would have bulges like a blacksnake that had visited the henhouse. We hoped the bulges were made by apples and even store-bought oranges or tangerines, but there might be an onion to suggest that our goodness could have been betterness.

Christmas Dinner on Rippy Hill meant a gathering of aunts and uncles and cousins to share a feast when my grandmother called out that "the fatted calf is on the scaffold high." Actually, it was usually fried chicken (drumsticks for the kids) and ham accompanied by large bowls of Irish and sweet potatoes plus vegetables put up in Mason jars last summer. A big bowl of butter, cornbread and biscuits, pies and cakes rounded out the menu—and the celebrants.

Instead of a buffet line and TV trays, we ate in shifts at the big dining table. The kids were not served first, nor allowed to grab the best goodies as I see so often nowadays. We were given what we were to eat, and we ate it—all of it. Dessert went only to members of the clean plate club—and we ate it from that same plate!

There were more presents to be opened after the clan gathered. One year a rule was made that if you got clothing you had to try it on. I still remember the commotion that ensued when one of my aunts pulled on a new pair of underpants. I can assure you that nothing vital was revealed—I was watching!—but that rule went away for some reason. We always got clothes, but we boys were more interested in a new pocketknife or some marbles.

I have celebrated many Christmases over the years, some all by myself on a far away Air Force base, some with only my wife and far from our families, but most with as many of family and friends as could be gathered. As the emphasis shifted from self to others and from Santa to Christ, Christmas became more meaningful. But it is no more important or memorable than those early ones on Rippy Hill.

The Prime Time
January 2002

The name of this newspaper is an assertion that for us older folks these are the best years of our lives. It is an affirmation of our worth and our importance, and a challenge to make the most of these retirement years.

We might be living in our last house, driving our last car, looking at our last TV, and so on. For this reason, the commercial world has already written us off, thinking that we will not be buying any more of their stuff. Well, it ain't necessarily so, as Spo'tin' Life sings so slyly in *Porgy and Bess.* One of my friends has just finished rebuilding a hot car that had languished in his garage for two decades. Another has acquired a high-performance sailplane, and another has started piano lessons. Many of us ARE upgrading our computers, buying new digital cameras, new cars, new digital TVs, and so on. After all, it is the American way . . .

Others are climbing mountains, seeing the world, acting in plays, writing their memoirs, or making a difference by serving on committees and giving of themselves in ways that help other people live better. Maybe they are not adding much to the Gross National Product, but what they are doing is also the American way. Some of us are always there to help when bad things happen to people.

For those of us who still enjoy good health and income, the later years bring us many opportunities to grow, learn, share, work, play, love, sing, listen, eat, see, ponder, walk, laugh, read, write, build, and enjoy. I left out a dozen good things and two dozen bad things we might do, no doubt. But I do think that our life is pretty much what we make it: what we decide to do, and our response to the things that happen to us, determine what our life will be like.

Are we a joy to others, or just to ourselves? Do we give thought to what we might do to make another person happy, or do we think mostly about what might make us happy? My grandfather advised me that in selecting a wife I should try to find a helpmeet, not just a help eat. Well, I got lucky (what man has sense enough to select a good wife? Right when he needs it most, Mother Nature contrives to rob him of any ability for rational judgment!) — the woman who has devoted nearly fifty years of her life to making mine super great, is obviously more than a helpmeet.

Each year I resolve to try real hard to be as good a husband to her as she is wife to me. Being a man, I fail more than I succeed in this endeavor. Yes, I do things around the house and take her out to eat sometimes, but I also spend a lot of time trying to be a good Lion and helping my county Historical Association live up to its charter.

Maybe this year will be better. But it is up to me to make it happen in my life, and it is up to you to make it happen in yours. We gotta decide very day and every hour what is most important, and then do that. We men know that our ladies will help us, for they really do want to be proud of us (after all, they selected us, too, you know!) but let's do our part to make their job easier. It takes more than a little peck on the cheek and a pat on the latter part of their wonderful anatomy as we head out the door. Maybe sometimes we should not go, but stay and tend the little fire that started in a couple of hearts so many years ago.

Ah, Romance!
February 2002

During my short tenure with *Prime Times!* our editor has selected "Romance" as a possible topic for February each year. I suppose that is because it contains Valentine's Day. I told Madalyn last year that if I could write about romance I would be rich, and I sent her an account of my taking my cow to visit the bull when I was a young lad with no inkling of what was about to happen to her. Madalyn printed it anyway, with a drawing of a smiling cow.

Anne has offered an alternate choice this year, but I don't remember what it is. Besides, I got good response to my approach to Home Décor, about which I know very little, so I think I will address the subject of Romance, about which I know very little more. How can I do this? Easy. I have some experience with it.

Seeing my attention shift to a young woman walking by, one of my engineering colleagues asked me how long I had been so interested in girls. Without hesitation I replied, "Ever since I found out they are not boys!"

This discovery occurred before I started to school, when we moved to live near a cousin. I came from the city, and she was a farm girl. She knew everything, and I knew nothing of value in my new environment of animals and plants. But she was nice about telling me not to eat those red berries or not to wade in the mud puddle barefoot because I would get the "toe itch." I came to like being with her.

When I started to school there were both boys and girls, but I played with the boys at recess. There was one girl who had long brown hair and read poems and things with a lilting voice that made me notice her. The more I noticed, the more I liked. Soon I was telling my mother about Phyllis, and thinking about her a lot. But there was no reason to do any more than that.

In the third grade, there was blonde Evelyn, who invited me into her house one day on our way home from school. We went up into the attic, where the only light came through the window from which we surveyed the street. She looked so pretty that I stole a kiss, then bolted out of her house and ran all the way home. She joined me on our walk home many more times before I moved away. Now I wonder whether she wanted me to do that again . . .

And so it went. There was always one girl that was special to me, but she never knew about it, mainly because I did not know what to do about her. So I did nothing. Then all of my friends were dating and even marrying, and I still did nothing. A young woman walked into my presence one day at church, and I finally decided I had better do something. Why? Well, she looked nice, she walked nice, she sounded nice, and she even smelled nice. Add big brown eyes and a sweet smile, and I just could not let this one get away . . .

I remember a little couplet that I saw about that time: "How can I face love's deeper dart / When merely holding one small hand uses up all my heart?" If you don't understand that, then read no farther. I don't know any better way to describe what happens when that special someone enters your consciousness. All senses become more sensitive to every nuance of whatever that person does. The rustle of her skirt, the little bounce of her hair when she walks, the sparkle in her eyes when they meet yours—sensory overload! Every thought is either *of* her, or colored by thoughts *about* her.

Is this romance? You tell me. It took me about a week to fall hopelessly, helplessly in love with this happy person who walked on air and whose voice fell so gently on my ears. It took about another week for it to happen to her, and then we began to make plans for a future together. That future has been 48 years so far, all but one as man and wife.

Sometimes the realization that this woman was giving her life to me was overwhelming. How can I be worthy of this? Can I ever live up to her expectations and my responsibilities? Ah, but in that first flush of romantic togetherness, these considerations could wait. Remember guys, if you did not want this one to get away, you must always see that she never wants to. She will help you with this, if you will just pay attention.

Dance
March 2002

Hey, this is starting to be fun! Writing about things I don't know anything about, I mean. It is actually easier because I don't have to get anything right or verify any facts.

My first experience with dance came when one of my high school teachers took it upon herself to see that we ALL had fun at our social gatherings. Miss Wages was an athletic woman with a lot of energy and enthusiasm, but getting ANY boys on the floor for round dancing to her records was nearly impossible, even for her. So she decided that she would teach all of us to square dance, and made this activity a part of her Phys. Ed. classes.

It certainly was good aerobic exercise (unheard of then), but the best part was that we got to take the girls' hands and sometimes even put our arms around their waists. It was a revelation to me that the girls were not all soft; some of them were downright muscular! But they all smiled a lot and seemed to enjoy the dancing as much as we did.

As prom time approached, we boys became more willing to try round dancing. Here we could use our good right arm to pull a willing partner in close while trying not to step on her feet. By then the more talented guys were doing the jitterbug to lively music, but many of us were just plodding around, trying to hear the beat hidden somewhere under a slow melody and to steer away from the other couples. With all this concentration on externals there was little chance to gaze into her eyes or even appreciate the light brush of her hair on our cheek.

I never did get the hang of it, for my wife says that dancing with me is somewhat akin to being paired with a Mack truck. I had to do a turn with our daughter at her wedding, but since she is an accomplished dancer, there was no disgrace. Must have done OK, because one of her friends asked me to dance with her, and then her mother did, and then my sister-in-law, and well, it got to be a pretty nice party . . .

Our adopted daughter's biological mother was a dancer, and Sharon showed her own talent very early by moving in synch with anything rhythmic that she heard. We started her in ballet school as soon as they would take her, and she was indeed a natural. She later went on *pointe* without any difficulty and her feet never bothered her. We even moved so that she could walk to the Academy of Ballet every day. She loved to dance, and we loved to see her and her friends dance.

Unfortunately, she broke a little bone in her foot (known as the "ballerina break") twice, neither time while dancing. The long healing times set her back, but that is not why she gave up the ballet. When the yearbooks came out near the end of her junior year of high school, she suddenly realized that when she graduated her entry would have only her name, with no activities associated with it. So she asked whether I would mind if she took only a few dance classes so that she could do other things after school.

Sharon was one of Tevye's daughters in *Fiddler*, made a name for herself writing for the school paper, and still enjoyed dancing with her friends at the Academy. Dance is many things to many people, but it certainly brings a lot of pleasure both to those who dance and to those who are better at watching others do it.

Our Environment
April 2002

The Thesaurus offers so many words for environment that just listing them would provide a third of my column space. Given that much leeway, I can easily comply with our editor's topic of the month. Again!

When we are choosing our personal environment, there is much we can control, but probably more that we cannot. We might choose a place with a good climate if we like outdoor activities, but we cannot control the weather. We might choose a nice house in a nice neighborhood, but one of those neighbors might make us want to move somewhere else. We might like to sleep with our windows open, but there are many noisemakers out there that can make us close them, or maybe pull the covers over our heads.

In the city we have traffic and the sirens of emergency vehicles to help us sleep. In the country, we get to hear the incessant buzzing of the cicadas in season, and the birds that whistle at us in the morning. One bird insists that he wants "Tea, too!" when I add water to the birdbath, and another screams continually for "Pierce, Pierce!" even though Charlie Pierce moved away years ago. Once we lived near a tidewater pond inhabited by several mallard families. Those ducks loved to party at night, and they must have had a great storyteller among them, for the stillness of early morning was frequently shattered by their raucous laughter as they all joined in the fun. Since I went to work early, I did not care to party with them.

What is important to us changes as we become more comfortable, as more of our fundamental needs are taken care of. A starving person will not be concerned about whether his fork is from the same pattern as his spoon. A homeless person will not care whether windows have shades or drapes. Nor will it matter whether his coat goes with his pants or his belt matches his shoes. It is only when our real needs are met that we consider such niceties.

Many Americans enjoy the luxury of retirement. The fundamentals are assured, so we can turn our attention to the things that make our lives pleasant and fun. But do we ever consider what our good life may cost our grandchildren, our neighbors, and our planet? It is not only the meek who shall inherit the earth we leave behind; everybody will!

Does it matter whether your motor vehicle gets 40 miles to the gallon or 20? Whether it is carefully tuned to burn its fuel cleanly? Whether you recycle stuff or put out two or more big cans of trash every week? Whether you pay the minimum water bill each month? Whether you are a good neighbor? Whether you are taking more than you are giving? Whether you have the biggest or the best? Whether you are first or last? All of these considerations impact our environment, believe it or not.

Environment is not just the air, light, water and earth that sustain us. Our modern civilization has done more to harm that part than to help it, I believe. The same "civilization" of us savage beasts should have made the neighborhood part better, but has it? We don't seem to get along any better now than our forebears did in Biblical times. We know more about everything now than anyone ever did, but we seem to use only what brings us pleasure and ignore the rest.

With all of our knowledge, have we missed the understanding part? How long will our abused earth sustain us? How long can we expect to live in a world where hatred looms larger than love? If we believe that all the darkness in the world cannot hide the light of one small candle, dare we hope that by learning to love we might light more candles?

Turbo, the Supercharged Cat
May 2002

This subject is easy, too, except for keeping it short enough to be a column instead of a book. I have been associated with animals all of my life and have written several columns about them over the years.

I had a small dog before I had a brother. Later as young boys, he had a dog and I had a cat. From then on, he always had a dog, and I have always had at least one cat. I also had a Jersey cow as a pet; she belonged to my grandmother, and was obtained from the Biltmore herd to supply milk for our families. I made a pet of her by brushing her coat periodically with the mule's currycomb and spending more time with her than just that required to milk her.

Our son Thomas was in the Air Force he married and was thus able to have cats at his house. He named them Porsche, Turbo and Carrera for the sports car he admired. Porsche was a timid little Siamese female who loved everybody, and always piled on Turbo to sleep. She died too young of cancer.

We have Carrera now, and I wrote about her last year (see p.20).

Turbo was the classic inquisitive and playful little tomcat who never really grew up. He enjoyed people and play as long as he lived. He was striped like a tiger, but had a lot of white on his face, legs and entire underside. He was well traveled, having lived in Texas and Virginia as well as Polk and Henderson counties. He was neutered and his front paws were declawed early on so he would be a harmless housecat. But he did love to hunt, so he was allowed outside. I was afraid he would not be able to defend himself, but he showed us that he could climb trees and catch squirrels and voles as well as any cat. He also was quick enough to bat a diving bird out of the sky when it pecked him on the back.

He grew large, but was always gentle with us and the other cats. His loud purring (hence the name, Turbo) was reassuring to them, I guess. He learned to let himself out by leaping up to hit the screen door latch handle with his front paws and landing in the yard when the door swung open from his momentum. He literally hit the ground running, and his tail was usually up as he checked out the shrubs and then the woods. He was not afraid of anything and seemed to enjoy everything.

Often I would be working at my drawing table when someone opened the door for Turbo to come back in from his hunt. He was usually pink from rolling in the dust of our Polk County red clay, and I learned to cover my drawing quickly before he arrived. He would bound down the hall and leap up onto my table, touch his nose to mine in greeting, then flop down and roll over to have his pink tummy rubbed. I really did not want him up there in his dusty condition, but I just learned to deal with it, because he was such a winsome rascal. How could one resist his *joie de vivre* and rattling purr?

Turbo's life was cut short by a disease he picked up outdoors. We always allowed our pet cats to go out because they enjoyed it so much and seemed to be "in their element" outside. But we have finally learned the lesson the hard way enough times that we now agree that if you love your housecat, you must see that he stays inside. Then play with him and groom him enough to compensate somewhat for his lack of freedom. A long, quiet life inside for my cat is preferable, at least to me, to a violent and untimely end outside.

Ancestors
June 2002

    This one may be a little more difficult to write about. Might have to think about it and learn some things. Synonyms for Ancestor don't help much in this case. *Forebears* I have none; not even kin to the famous Three. I do have to watch about griping, though, as my dear wife does not like it any better than Mama Bear did. I used to be able to climb the mountain like a goat, but there are no *forerunners* that I am aware of. And since this is a family newspaper, I will not look for *progenitors*, as we don't talk about things like that in polite company. In other papers and on TV, yes, but not in *Prime Times!* even though we are thought to be a "mature audience."

    Now what? Some of my friends have traced their ancestors to the time of the Norman Conquest (the only historical date I remember besides 1492 and 1776; that was in 1066). I know about one grandfather's grandfather, who is supposed to have come over here from Dublin, and is called Irish Edward Rippy. However, my Aunt Mildred did not find any Rippys in Ireland when she inquired while visiting there. I think my grandmother is Scot-Irish, and I know my father's people are all English. If they ever did anything to distinguish themselves from other hard-working people, I am not aware of it.

So I am a WASP. I am also a Tar Heel and a Baptist. All of this used to be GOOD. Now we are no longer politically correct and are becoming a minority in the country we largely founded, on what were thought to be excellent principles. They did work for a while, though, and I think it is too bad that our wonderful Constitution is now being used against us. Many in "the Media" are making a mockery of all that my generation fought and died to defend. I used to say that "being a Baptist is sort of like being a Tar Heel; there is just not much you can do about it." It is not funny any more.

My wife Fran got some fancy software for her computer to help her trace and record her ancestry. With help from her mother and a cousin, she filled in a lot of blanks and produced several pages of family tree printout. When I got a new computer and gave her my old one, we could never get the data to load into the same software when she installed it. With so much labor lost, she is not trying to find more ancestors right now.

One of Fran's grandfathers was a Cherokee, but neither she nor her mother can prove it. Since he chose not to take part in the "Trail of Tears," there is no official record that he was born. A brick mason, he helped to build several notable buildings in central Texas. Since Fran is more Cherokee than a recent Chief of the Eastern Band is, I would like to prove it, so she can collect whatever the Cherokee are entitled to. Ha!

We gave our children Christian names honoring family and the people in the Bible. We wanted to give them names to live up to, not to have to live down. We believe that they have more than done so, and they have given good names to their children as well. The family reunions are not as well attended now, because everyone is so "busy" these days, but we still keep it touch on birthdays and Christmas at least. And e-mail!

So that is what genealogy is about. We are products of a big and diverse gene pool that even so produces a few nuts to enrich the mix. Every family history is part Soap Opera with its own stories of triumph and tragedy, good times and bad. We are all kin to folks with whom we are pleased to share a name, and others about whom we wonder how they got that way. The thing is, they probably wonder about us, too!

School Days in the 30s and 40s
July 2002

I remember those "dear old golden rule days" very well, where we learned a lot more than "readin,' writin,' and 'rithmatic." I was "taught to the tune of a" ruler applied to the palm of my hand, never "a hickory stick." I loved most of my teachers and liked most of my classmates, so while I got As and Bs in the subject matter, I got mostly Cs and Ds in what was called either "Conduct" or "Deportment" on our report cards. I never got deported, but I did have to "stay in" a lot.

We offenders were then allowed to dust the erasers, wash the blackboard, or write "I will not . . ." two hundred times. Some learned to hold two pencils together and thus write two lines at the same time. Before you get to feeling righteous, be aware that Thomas Jefferson had a machine on his desk that linked two pens together so that he could write a second original on an adjacent sheet of paper. Great minds . . .

At home I had toys and a too-young brother to play with. At school there were both girls and boys, but we segregated ourselves for play except when the teacher led games that got everyone involved. The girls jumped rope and played hopscotch; we boys played marbles and tag or some kind of ball game during our favorite period: recess! I now think that a reason we did not play with girls was not because it was "sissy," but because many of them could outrun and outjump us!

Since I never figured out which end of a ball to hold, I was not chosen by either team captain to play on his side. Seeing this, my second grade teacher made me the umpire for a baseball game. I thought it was because my Uncle Wallace played on the local pro team. I could not see anything without my thick glasses, so my father roared with laughter when I proudly told him about it. It was many years before I figured out why.

The girls wore dresses, many made from flour sacks, and the boys wore short pants and knit shirts to school. Most went barefoot except in the bitterest cold of winter. School was let out for a month or so for fall harvest, and we always got a day off to go to the Fair!

In the middle grades we boys changed to cloth shirts and long pants (or bib overalls, called "overhauls" by those who wore them), and one mother got her son to keep his shirttail tucked in by sewing lace to the hem! The girls became taller than the boys and some of them began to round out in places. This went unnoticed by most of the boys, but not for long. As we also got taller and got "muscles," we began to appreciate that the girls were, well, GIRLS. I wanted so much to grow biceps, but while they got hard and I could do chin-ups OK, mine never really bulged. Some of the other guys began to look like Superman without making any special effort. Did anyone say that life is fair?

There were many more changes in store when we entered high school. A first for us was a man teacher, but he was no novelty. Mr. Beach was a large man who addressed all of us as Mr. Smith and Miss Jones from day one, as if we were adults. It worked! We stood taller, answered respectfully, and faithfully observed all the new courtesies he quietly imposed on the class. He was also our coach, and we had to sing "Stout Hearted Men" as we did our warm-up calisthenics. His fine tenor voice was truly inspiring as we worked to build our muscles.

WWII was over by the time we graduated, and we had three returning veterans in our class. We also had a young married woman among us for a while. The guys exchanged knowing looks and smirks whenever she came or went, as if we knew something about her. We did not know the half of it, and after nearly fifty years of marriage, I still don't. And I don't think any other man does, either.

We were almost a family in our small school because everyone knew everyone else and their families. We scattered after graduation, but many of us are right back here. We enjoy seeing one another now because we bonded long ago without realizing it then. That is why class reunions are well attended, former teachers are honored, and everyone who gathers feels good for weeks afterward.

Wilbur Was Right!
August 2002

What is a hobby supposed to be? I ask because many times what starts as an idle pastime becomes an obsession. By definition, a hobby is pursued outside of one's job and primarily for pleasure. I believe that the pleasure part is the only consistent thing in the hobby business. I mean, if it ain't fun, why do it?

I have dabbled in several things that might have become hobbies, but I decided early on that my interest was not as big as the projected cost in dollars and time: photography, model railroading, and oil painting, for examples. The things that took hold of me and never let go are airplanes and flying them, but I found ways to make both possible without going bankrupt.

When I was about eight years old, my father brought me a toy airplane with a cardboard wing and a metal propeller that turned freely on a nail. I would hold it out the car window and watch that propeller spin (no air conditioning in those days!) I liked to feel it lift itself against my hand when I pointed the nose up slightly. My dad must have thought it was a good investment, because then I did not squabble with my younger brother during our Sunday drives.

There was a ten-foot string tied in an eyelet in one wing tip, and the instructions said to whirl the plane around me by leading it with the string. With practice I learned to let it go behind me by putting my arm over my head as it went around. Then I could fly the plane for a long time without getting dizzy. I soon learned to land it on its little wheels and later to pull it up and over in a sort of loop-the-loop.

Then a real airplane began to appear in the sky near our house. It had two wings stacked one above the other, and I could see the people's heads when it came close. Naturally, I asked my dad if we could ride in that airplane, since I saw it several times every day. On Sunday afternoon we followed the airplane to its landing place on a big grass field. Soon my dad and I were strapped into the front cockpit, and then we were gathering speed across that big field.

I still remember the feeling of exhilaration that came over me when the wheels stopped bumping along and the ground began to drop away from us. I have never lost that tinge of awe and wonder as I have made hundreds of takeoffs in various kinds of airplanes over the years. If I am flying solo, I will sometimes bellow that "Wilbur was right!" I love the freedom the airplane gives me to go up or down, here or there, without regard to any sort of boundaries.

As I was growing up, I designed, built, and flew model airplanes. Then at sixteen I used earnings from a summer job to learn to fly with Oscar Meyer at the Hendersonville airport. When school reopened in the fall, I had to give up my summer job and the extra dollars it had provided for flying lessons, but I did get to fly solo before that happened. I later got my credentials both to design and to fly real airplanes, so one facet of my hobby (designing) became my livelihood, and enabled me to pursue the other part (flying).

I got my name on many airplanes, some great and some that never made it into production. I felt that I contributed something in every case, but I am especially pleased to have helped create the great Boeing 747 and the Navy's F8U, A-7 and the Super F-18 that is taking its place on the carriers now. The 747 is still in production after nearly 40 years, and the Blue Angels fly the F-18.

We used our airplanes to take vacations that covered more territory than we could have in a car, and I gave dozens of people their first airplane ride. But the most fun was just turning the plane every way but loose, doing loops, rolls and spins, and helping a friend get aerial photographs. I was the only pilot he flew with who would position the airplane correctly on the first pass, even though it might be about to fall out of the sky. And I just plain like to fly the airplane, from the thrill of the takeoff, to putting it back on the ground ever so gently even in tricky wind conditions.

I have never lost my enthusiasm for airplanes, and I was the only father my kids knew who looked forward to returning to work on Monday mornings.

Wildlife
September 2002

Having written about the animals we take into our homes as pets, we get to write about wild animals this month. For me, the "lions and tigers and bears, oh my!" are kindred spirits. I don't buy into my being descended from a monkey, though, for that is an insult to the monkey. But I might be part bear (I eat just about anything and pretty much do as I please) and I really would like to fly like an eagle. Or even a Great Egret . . .

The egrets used to come over and fish in the tidewater pool behind our house in Virginia. I viewed those big, beautiful birds through the eyes of an aeronautical engineer and pilot of airplanes. I loved to watch the downy feathers rise on the upper surface of their wings as they slowed for their landing in the shallow water. If they misjudged the water depth and got their tail feathers wet, they would make a sudden maximum performance take-off and then select a spot closer to shore. Sometimes they would arrange their large wings (about six feet in span) in the shape of a parachute to make a steep approach over our two-story house without building up too much speed for the landing. They are masters of the art and science of flight.

The little terns arrived in late May to take minnows from our pond. The terns hover with rapid wing beats about twenty feet above the water, then go down like a dive bomber to grab their meal. Of course they get wet, but they just shake the water off and beat their wings furiously to get airborne again before swallowing their catch and climbing back up to spot the next one. Commercial fishing boats employ small airplanes to find schools of fish in the ocean for them, by the way.

We watched for the Carolina Black Skimmers to arrive next, and would run out in the middle of supper to greet them. We all liked to see them swoop in and level off close enough to the smooth water surface to lay a little furrow in it with their beak. Then they would pull up and turn like a crop dusting airplane to go back down along the line in the water to snap up the minnows who came up to investigate. Their average was two minnows per pass.

Cable TV has brought wild animals right into the den with me. I was thrilled when our cable people announced that we were going to get Animal Planet, but I don't enjoy seeing crocodiles, anacondas, or cute little dogs doing unusual things in somebody's back yard. So I have to channel-surf to see the running cheetah, the bear waiting in midstream for a salmon to jump right into his mouth, mama lion teaching her playful cubs, the osprey plucking a big fish right out of the water on the fly, and the aerobatic courtship of eagles that lock talons and tumble about in the sky.

I enjoy watching all of them as they go about their business of survival, except when they eat what they have caught. Now that is another matter. We know that they are going to eat it, so why don't they just fade away like they did when lovers went into the clinch in the olden days? Nowadays the camera just keeps on rolling, both in the bedroom and in the jungle. I know that the graceful gazelle must die for the lion to live, but I don't want to see it.

Since I am not a plant (though my wife has decided that I am a computer potato) I must be animal. But there are differences between the other animals and me that are sometimes puzzling. Why do I have to get haircuts and my cat does not? Her hair grows to appropriate lengths on her face, back, and ears, and stops. She gets new points for her claws all the time, but because I am "kin," I have to cut my nails all the time. But at bath time, I think I get the better deal, IF I can get to a shower . . . Brings to mind what a human mother does when she discovers breakfast on her child's face on the way to church.

We have domesticated some animals so that they serve our needs and wants. Some animals devote their lives to us, and we take the lives of others. For some animals, it is a matter of our survival, but for other animals it is a simple matter of dominion. We take what we want because we can. I think there is a difference between the tiger who kills an antelope to eat, and a man who then takes the tiger's life just to have a trophy. He is no match for the tiger without his powerful rifle. For myself, I would rather capture the tiger on film and let him go on with his life. As long as I don't have to watch him eat.

One Man's Toys
October 2002

Our wonderfully creative editor lady has offered us "Toys Men Especially Love" as this month's theme. There are too many men and too many toys, all different, even to mention in a mere column. So I will tell you about some of the things that I like to play with.

My regular readers know that I like airplanes and cats. Even model airplanes and house cats will do. For me, a house cat is just a scaled down version of a tiger or a cougar. There was a cougar at the Griffith Park Observatory in California, always stretched out and fast asleep in his cage. Since his back was against the bars, I found it hard to resist reaching in and rubbing his tummy.

There are people who do get to play with big cats, as in the movie *Charlie, the Lonesome Cougar*, but I have had to settle for many little Charlies and Charlenes over the years. I helped some of them hone their cat skills as kittens. And they have stretched out next to me and let me rub their tummy as they slept.

I played with model airplanes first, but I did get to play with real ones, too. I justified having an airplane by taking the family places in it. I also justified practicing my pilot skills continually so that they could feel confident riding with me. I got so cocky at one point that I would stop by the airport on my way home from work, release the chain holding one wing, and if the wind gusts did not try to lift the wing away from me, I would just re-attach the chain and go on home. On most windy days I was the only fool flying an airplane off that field in Texas! By landing that plane successfully many times in every sort of bad wind condition, I was able to do it again once when my whole family was aboard. Had I not had all that fun playing with the wind in my little airplane, it might have been a different story that day in Mississippi.

After my wife Fran soldered together our first computer from a kit (she also built the electronic components of our first stereo system while I built the speaker cabinets) the guys who supervised this effort kept asking her what games I had acquired to play on the computer. She always had to report "None." Some years later, she realized that the games I play are called MS Publisher and Adobe Photoshop.

I really enjoy creating ads, signs and posters for her needlework shop and the organizations I am part of. I am finishing up a 24-page booklet right now. I also enjoy restoring old family photographs to presentable condition. I can remove spots, creases and scratches, remove glare on eyeglasses, and get rid of objectionable background clutter. Fran's mother sends snapshots and tells me to "remove those other people; I don't know who they are." So I just grab a big shrub from somewhere else and plant it there in the park where the strangers were standing.

I love the challenge of getting pianos to produce music, either by tuning and repairing them, or trying to play them. A big concert grand is especially rewarding, both to tune and to play. I once told a dealer who had set up his concert rental piano for one of our meetings that it sure was great to start a crescendo and not run out of piano before you got to the top of the phrase!

Another joy is driving a responsive sports car on our mountain roads. My MGB was equal to every curve and hill; the only problem was coming up behind a big ol' station wagon whose brake lights came on at curves that I could easily take at road speed. It got so frustrating that I finally sold the MG because I could not enjoy driving it any more.

My late brother was very good at playing baseball, and he also considered a 20-ton bulldozer a toy. I think one of those little 4-wheel skid loaders (one is called a Bobcat) would be fun to play with, but I have not found an opportunity to try it. One can do a lot of damage to a landscape quickly, even with one of those little things. Guess I'd better stick to my computer.

Here is my first draft of the column above that was actually published. There are enough differences that I think you might like to read this one, too! ☺

Toys Men Especially Love
(Not previously published)

There are too many men and too many toys, all different, even to mention in a mere column. So I am just going to tell you about some of the things that I like to play with. Since I am told that I am not a typical person (is anyone?) my toy choices will not match up with those of very many men.

I will start with airplanes and cats. Even model airplanes and house cats will do, if I cannot have the real thing. For me, a house cat is just a scaled down version of a tiger or a cougar. I cannot tell you how many times I saw that movie about "Charlie, the Lonesome Cougar."

When I was going to school on the GI bill in California we did not have any extra $$, but I did still have my big ol' Buick from USAF days. I would fill it with some of my fellow students (who helped fill the gas tank, too) and go somewhere that was free on Sunday afternoons. One such place was the Griffith Park Observatory. There was a cougar there, always stretched out and fast asleep in his cage. Since his back was against the bars, I found it hard to resist reaching in and rubbing his tummy. Don't think that was Charlie, but Charlie did look like him.

There are people who do get to play with big cats as pets, but I have had to settle for many, many little Charlies and Charlenes over the years. I have helped some of them learn cat skills as kittens separated from their mama too soon. And they have stretched out next to me and let me rub their tummy as they slept.

In the case of airplanes, I played with models first, but did get to play with real ones, too. I justified having an airplane by taking the family places in it. I also justified practicing my pilot skills continually in order for them to feel confident in riding with me. I got so cocky at one point that I would stop by the airport on my way home from work, release the chain holding one wing, and if the wind gusts did not try to lift the wing away from me, I would just re-attach the chain and go on home! On many windy days I was the only fool flying an airplane off that field!

By landing that plane successfully in every sort of bad wind condition, I was able to do it again once when my whole family was aboard. Had I not had all that fun playing with the wind in my little airplane, it might have been a different story that day in Mississippi.

When my wife Fran soldered together our first computer from a kit (she also built the electronic components of our first stereo system while I built the speaker cabinets) the guys who supervised this effort kept asking her what games I had acquired to play on the computer. She always had to report "NONE." Some years later, she realized that the games I play on my computer are called MS Publisher and Adobe Photoshop.

I really enjoy creating ads, signs and posters for her needlework shop and the organizations I am part of. I am finishing up a 24-page booklet right now. I also enjoy restoring old family photographs to presentable condition. I can remove spots and scratches, remove glare on eyeglasses, and get rid of objectionable background clutter. Fran's mother sends snapshots and tells me to "remove those other people; I don't know who they are." So I just grab a tree from somewhere else and plant it there in the park where the strangers were standing.

While my brother was very good at playing baseball, he also considered a 20-ton bulldozer a toy. I think one of those little 4-wheel skid loaders (one is called a Bobcat) would be fun to play with, but I have not found the opportunity to try one of them. One can do a lot of damage to a landscape quickly, even with one of those little things. Guess I'd better stick to my computer.

Toys for Women
November 2002

Here is another opportunity to write of something I know nothing about; however, I noticed that some women wrote about men's toys last time, so I claim equal opportunity. If you think I will write of "boy toys," or certain battery-operated devices that are not flashlights, then turn the page. We are not going there, here.

When I was young, most women did the cooking and sewing and the guys drove the trucks and tractors. I could not imagine a woman really loving cars or airplanes, boats or trucks. Nowadays, it appears to me that many women like the same toys that men do. They have even invaded some of our "macho" territory!

Flying a jet fighter for the Air Force, for instance. Can you imagine the reaction of an eager young male aviation cadet reporting for his first lesson in the jet airplane on seeing that his instructor is a *woman?* I was just as surprised when I was assigned to a lovely young woman for flight instruction! Jeannie really did love airplanes and flying, and she was good, too. As is Patty Wagstaff, who was an aerobatic champion before she hit the air show circuit. Gender is not a factor in flying airplanes.

One day while I was waiting for my car to be serviced, an Ann-Margret look-alike came over and sat in a nearby easy chair and struck up a conversation with me. Normally, the only young ladies who talk to me are those who are just doing their job, and it turned out that this one was, too. She wanted to sell me a new SUV. No hard sell, just conversation. She learned that I flew airplanes and I learned that she drove a big dump truck for several years and loved it.

When I lived in Virginia there were many huge "Virginian" dump trucks [two axles with dual tires on each side under the bed] on the road, and they all had signs on the back that said "DO NOT PUSH." I never tried that, but I did pass them at every opportunity. When I discovered that some of them were driven by young women, I always checked the driver out as I went by. One driver that I passed had beautiful, long blond locks, so I stole another glance as I got alongside. His beard was long and blond, too. Oh, well.

There are lots of diesel-powered pickups in my area that have dual rear wheels and are used to tow "fifth wheel" type horse trailers. As often as not, it is a diminutive gal who dismounts after skillfully parking the rig right where she wants it. What about four-wheel drive trucks and SUVs? Same deal. They love 'em!

What about guns? Macho male toys, right? Well, my great aunt Edna was a crack shot. She lived alone in the country, so that reputation was good security. Everyone saw her shoot mistletoe out of her trees with a .22 rifle, so there were no unwelcome visitors. My wife took riflery as an elective in college and she scored better than I had on the Air Force ranges. Our dentist's daughter was a national champion with her rifle, but she chose continuing her engineering training over going to the Olympics.

Are there any toys that only men play with? Or women? I hate to admit that I cannot think of any. I will have to read what the ladies have to say this time to get the answers, I suppose. Anyone wanna bet there are not any gender toys any more?

The Folly of Prophecy
December 2002

Prophecy by non-prophets is apparently doomed to failure. I know, because I wrote the Prophecy for my high school graduating class. Absolutely none of it came true; not even close! She did not marry him. The one predicted to have five marriages in as many years has one husband and a fine family. I guess all of my predictions were considered harmless, because I have not been sued—yet.

Upon reflection, I realize that I did have a glimmer of success: the one I said would become an executive of a lumber company actually served one as their accountant. And while I planned then to go to college, I did wind up serving Uncle Sam as I predicted. Now that you know my meager qualifications as a prophet, will you read what I predict for our future?

What I have seen in the 55 intervening years is that while technology continually delivers totally unexpected miracles, people have not changed at all. Not for as long as anything has been recorded about us. Sure, we may look and dress a little different, but we act the same. The Bible attests abundantly to that; every conceivable activity of man has been reported and the consequences spelled out. If you won't accept it from that source, then how about the writings of Shakespeare and the ancient Greeks before that?

Therefore I predict that people generally will be no better or worse than they are now. The fat people will want to be skinny, and the skinny ones will want to put on some weight. The ones with no hair will want hair, and the ones with abundant curly hair will want it to be straight. While one may hate his job, another would be glad just to have a job. The one with two cars will want yet another, and a boat, too, while the one with no car would settle for a reasonable bus schedule. So there will always be striving. And people will love each other and kill each other with equal enthusiasm.

When we first heard about cloning, we fantasized that we could send our clone to work and go to the beach. If we got into trouble, we could send our clone off to jail while we continued our good life. Of course it went from bad to worse, because we figured a woman could clone herself and make a lot of money without having to . . . well, that may be why the government is trying to prevent cloning of humans!

I suppose NASA will send people farther into space, a la Star Trek, but right now they are trying to convince the last holdouts that they actually sent some guys to the moon. We had a moon walk watch party at our house, and by the time they actually did it, it was an anti-climax because they had already showed us so much computer simulation to fill the long wait. Our small children were unimpressed and went right back to bed. One of our guests left his shoes in the entry hall, and was surprised to see them there two weeks later.

We have surpassed all the wonders predicted by visionaries of the past. I expect that our actual technical achievements will continue to go beyond our wildest dreams. What we do with these discoveries and new abilities is up for grabs. One of my friends is actively pursuing bringing the fruits of the budding field of nanotechnology to Our Area. What are we talking about here? It involves the manipulation of atoms to build materials, machines and devices. What will it be good for? As Marconi retorted, "What good is a baby?"

What indeed. I am sure that today's babies, our grandchildren, are going to be just like us, but will live in a world far different from the one we know. I hope that they will be happy in it.

Money!
January 2003

St. Paul advised Timothy that "the love of money is the root of all evil." English author Samuel Butler later wrote that "the *want* of money is . . ." The synonyms and expressions for money are too numerous to count, and every quotable person has had something to say about it. So what can a pore ol' country boy say that has not already been said better?

This fool is going to rush in with his Word machine anyway. I like money. Doesn't everyone? The photographers who used to ask us to say "Cheese!" are now suggesting we say "Money!" We like the idea of being given money, but parting with it is another matter. It depends on why we are being asked to.

Does anyone pay his taxes with a smile? I tried it, but they wanted money (OK, so I saw it on a sign in our local tax office. Do you expect me to think up all-new material?) On the other hand, there are things and causes that will have me grinning while parting with real dollars. You, too, right?

Before we kids started playing Monopoly, we made play coins from the "holes" we punched out of baby chick boxes. Since the punchings were all the same size, we would write numbers on them to make nickels and dimes etc. Did you ever swap a younger kid a nickel for his dime because it was bigger and he'd think he had more money? Of course not.

When I was about ten (1940) I was given an allowance of 25 cents. I don't think it was related to whether I had done my chores well; Mother just gave me a quarter at the end of the month. That made me very happy, and I would head downtown with that quarter tied into the corner of my handkerchief so I would not lose it.

At Kress's or Woolworth's I could buy a model airplane kit for 10 cents. With my fourteen cents change came a store coupon with numbers on the corners. The penny sales tax I had paid would cover some 33 cents in purchases, so the clerk had torn off a corner of the coupon that had a "10" on it. I think there was another ten and two fives on the other three corners. When I bought a nickel glider (much larger than the penny ones and they flew better,) I presented my nickel and the coupon, and the five corner was removed. You can believe I saved those sales tax coupons as long as they had corners.

Many people today will not stoop to pick up a dime, let alone a penny. I still do. An older friend does, too. He told me that he picked up two pennies on his way into a car salesroom where he easily paid some $45,000 cash for his new car. The young salesmen were laughing when he got inside, and he discovered that they were seeding the lot just to see who would pick up the shiny coppers. Who had the last laugh?

My daughter, when younger, used to say, "But Daddy, it is ONLY twenty dollars!" and I had no way to explain to her that for me there is no such thing as ONLY twenty dollars. I have built-in "sticker shock" when looking at new cars—our first HOUSE cost a lot less than cars do today. I used to carry a folded dollar bill hidden in my wallet for emergencies like a flat tire, running out of gas, or getting hungry the day before payday. Over the years the number on that folded bill has had to get bigger and bigger. Too bad.

Our Government has been trying to stop making pennies for years. They had to change the material when the copper cost more than a penny. Our money is now so worthless that none of our coins can be made of traditional materials in any useful size. Upon hearing someone described as a "penny pincher," your great-grandchild is going to ask you, "What is a penny?" Too bad.

Some Questions
February 2003

Since reading Martha Sach's [fellow columnist at *Prime Times!*] recent columns about the wonders of our government, I have some questions, too. Since I am taking medicine for both stroke and high blood pressure, it is not good for me to think very much about our governments at any levels. And since I refuse to run for office even when begged (I might be elected!), I feel that I should not be loudly critical of those who do throw their hat into the ring and then try to make a difference. But I will ask anyway.

First question: Why are the victims of the WTC disaster worth so much more than members of our armed services, who go where they are sent and often do not come back?

Why did we allow members of Congress to opt out of Social Security in order to give themselves better retirement benefits than all but the wealthiest Americans? To add insult to injury, they forced the Amish people, who take care of their own, to pay Social Security taxes into a system which they definitely do not need, and which is probably the worst "return on investment" anywhere?

Whatever happened to the citizen legislator? Should not they be like the citizen soldier, who responds in time of need and then goes back home? Most members of Congress have never met a payroll and cannot drive a car or shop for groceries. They only go back home to campaign for re-election. Even if they do leave office, their exorbitant pensions mean that they become leeches on society instead of contributing members.

Could we get an amendment passed that would provide that no lawyer could serve in any law-making body because it is a conflict of interest? Just a thought.

Instead of cutting taxes, why not fund the National Park Service and the Geodetic Survey people? The Park Service must depend on volunteers to maintain trails and has had to close or severely limit access to some park areas because they do not have the funds for adequate staffing. Our

Topographic maps are so hopelessly out of date that they are nearly useless. These are legitimate functions of government that have been shortchanged for decades.

Why is it that the money you sacrificed to put aside for a rainy day won't even buy a decent umbrella when that day finally comes? Another service provided by our benevolent government.

Now you see why I try not to think about our government. This is no longer the country I learned to love as a boy and served in the USAF during the Korean War. The ideals I was taught are now ridiculed and the Constitution I defended has been misinterpreted almost beyond recognition. The melting pot has been cast aside to promote "diversity." What happened to "one nation, under God"? I try to be optimistic and at least appear to be a good-humored person, but nowadays I find myself thinking that I am glad to be old because I won't see much more of this relentless destruction of my country.

With all that off my chest, I will now pose some questions of less gravity:

Why are they called "apartments" when "togetherments" would be more descriptive of life in them? Waiting for the other shoe to drop is not just an expression.

Why does a big semi-trailer truck pull out to pass another one on a hill, and then creep up the hill alongside the other truck, effectively blocking the Interstate until they both reach the top? And even then they do not pull over immediately to let the bottled up traffic pass. Perhaps they do it for the same reason young women wear those short tops that reveal their flat tummies: because they CAN.

Why do we have to wait so much longer when we get in the shortest line?

Why does the person you have waited fifteen minutes in line to talk to get a phone call when your turn comes, then answer it and talk to them instead?

I have noticed many times that the department stores will advertise "All Bras Half Off," and when I check the accompanying photos, the ladies have both sides cinched up as tight as a saddle on a horse. Give us guys a break,
will ya?

Many restaurants have signs that read, "No shoes, No shirt, No service." I wonder what would happen if I showed up without my pants?

Now I am smiling again. I hope you are, too.

Winter: BAH-AH!
March 2003

I don't know which is worse, winter or August. Probably August, because we can usually wear enough clothes to keep warm in winter, but even after taking all of them off, it is still August.

Spring is wonderful as it brings new life, summer is OK if we don't have to work outside, and fall is beautiful with all the color. But by the time winter settles in, most of the trees and shrubs are bare, the sky is often bleak, and once-beautiful snow lingers on as messy slush or dangerous ice.

Many Americans live in good houses that protect them from these extremes of weather and enable them to live in comfort the year around. That is, as long as they don't have to go outside and Reddy Kilowatt (symbol and logo of the electric power companies in mid century) stays on the job. Ah, we take so much for granted nowadays!

I am not very good at being weathered in. If the power stays on, then we are warm and I can work at the computer, so I actually enjoy it. For a while. But if the power goes off, then there is no computer, no TV, and pretty soon not much warmth. Life then goes back about a hundred years to wood fires and oil lamps. We can cook because we use natural gas, so we eat pretty well even when ol' Reddy says he just cannot make it to our house today.

It is an adventure in primitive living. For a day or so. Then it starts to get tedious. We flip the switch from habit, but the light does not come on. We put stuff from the fridge into the garage, where we hope it will not freeze. We check the paper box and the mailbox, and usually find that those wonderful folks have managed to get to us, which brightens our day.

But I find that I can drink just so much hot chocolate and read just so much of that book I was trying to finish.

My dear wife Fran reads contentedly, plays solitaire (I do not do games), cross-stitches, writes letters, straightens up her closet and the kitchen cabinets, chats on the phone, and generally makes the best of it. Not me. I pace the floor, look out the window, go downstairs to the shop, come back up to see what there is to eat, mess with the fireplace, look out the window some more, and generally drive Fran crazy. She will finally say that she does not care how many little birds are at the feeder, or whether the water would re-freeze in the birdbath if I chipped the ice out and replaced it. Humph! I didn't want to go out there anyway.

She suggests that I straighten out my closet, "do something" with the stuff piled on my desk, write a letter, call a friend, and so on, *ad nauseam*. I don't want to hear about it. I just want outa here!

As long as Reddy Kilowatt stays ready and the little red Saturn can go up and down our driveway several times a day (or at least ONCE!) I can deal with winter. That means that I can write my columns, design and deliver camera-ready ads, tune a few pianos, go to Lions Club meetings, see our friends at the Post Office and Hardees, and do all the other things that fill our retirement years with satisfaction. Uh, spring IS just around the corner, isn't it?

I cannot find a column for April 2003, so either I did not write one, or I failed to log it into my computer! G.

Mother
May 2003

Of all the many observances and holidays which man has devised for his leisure or spiritual betterment, one of the most widely observed is Mother's Day. Every mother hopes to be remembered in some special way on this day.

Wherever kids are gathered, the leaders always plan something for Mother's Day. As far back as I can remember we picked a flower, drew one with crayons or made one of construction paper. My fourth grade teacher had us make a little booklet of verses about Mother, and a classmate helped me draw a fancy border on the cover of mine. Even we of limited talent could thus do right by our mothers.

I think that my mother was a good mother. She was born in 1900 and died in 1970. She was married for ten years, widowed when her boys were eight and four years old. Urged by some of the family to put us in an orphanage, she refused and set about raising us herself. She cooked, washed and ironed for us—no machines for those tasks in our house—while working a full time job. Years later, when we each offered her a home with us, she opted for an apartment near her church.

Mother's old and dear friends ask me to write about her. It is easy and interesting to write about characters like my Uncle Ethan, but what can I write about a woman who lived mostly for others and met her responsibilities squarely? Who was always there for whoever needed help with living or dying? Who loved one man with all her heart, and never uttered a negative word about him as long as she lived? Whose life was shortened because when she could not buy both shoes for her boys and medicine for her high blood pressure, you know where the money went?

I think that my wife Fran is a good mother, too. We adopted a boy and a girl when they did not come naturally because she convinced me that a home needs children to be complete. She has made every house a home for all of us over the years. Her steadfast love binds us all—from four very different gene pools—into a family. Hers is the voice of calm and wisdom when the yelling starts. She asks little and gives much. My grandfather had advised me to seek a wife that would be "a help-meet, not just a help-eat," but I had no idea when I fell victim to her sweet smile and dancing eyes that Fran could cook, too.

Now I want to tell you about the mother who was part of the package when I married. A marriage joins two families, not just two people, for better or worse, and all have a part in determining which it will be. After I asked Fran's father for her hand in marriage, her mother Marguerite began a program to prepare two kids for setting up housekeeping in a far country.

I took Fran to California, where she toiled at a job to supplement my GI Bill, and turned our little rented cottage into a great meeting place for my fellow students and me to do homework together. I feel that I made an excellent choice in Fran, but our mothers were not so sure at first. I guess all mothers hope that their offspring will do better than that.

I am truly grateful for having another family, especially since most of mine is gone. No one goes to Texas in the middle of summer by choice, but all of my family made the trek to help celebrate Marguerite's 85th birthday. She received us kindly, and the rest of her family did, too. I never feel like an "in-law" there, for by her example, Marguerite's family has become my family.

It occurred to me long ago that each of us should honor our *mother* on our birthday—for surely it is a day she remembers well! The Commandment to honor our parents is the only one containing a promise: that our days may be long upon the earth. But I am reminded of a sign in a little country gas station that said, "We HONOR all major credit cards, but we only accept CASH." Honor? Let's be sure to give Mom the real thing, and often. So guys, tell all the mothers in your life. But if you aren't much with words, the florists stand ready to help.

My Dad, My Hero
June 2003

My father was born six months before the airplane, and lived a pretty full life before he married at age 25. He was kept at home to work so much that he completed only the fifth grade of school. His father bought the sanitary landfill at East Durham (NC) and made my Dad and Sam plow it repeatedly to prepare it for growing crops. Both Dad and the horse hated the stench. I don't know what became of Sam, but my Dad finally revolted and left home for good.

He had learned to ride motorcycles at age 15 and was racing them professionally for Harley-Davidson in Havana by age 19. When repair of injuries sustained in a racing accident cost him most of his savings, he decided to look for a less dangerous line of work. He signed on with a crew surveying an alternate site for the Panama Canal. Working in dense jungle, they were told not to pick up anything they dropped. One of the men automatically reached for his pencil and came up with a brightly colored little snake attached to his finger. He was dead before he could be helped, so Dad decided again that it was time to move on.

He got work on a freighter headed for China, and later weathered a storm with heavy seas washing over the deck and more lightning and fierce winds than he had ever heard of. On shore leave on the Chinese mainland, he had to flee some sort of uprising. They gave him a .45 automatic pistol and a Chinese boy to keep reloading its ammunition clips as they ran back toward the docks, firing at their pursuers. He made it back to the ship and it sailed to Hawaii.

Dad liked the islands and enlisted in the U.S. Army there. He was assigned to Battery A, 8th Field Artillery, and learned trigonometry so well that he was soon promoted and was teaching other gunners how to aim the artillery pieces. He played a lot of baseball and enjoyed touring the islands. Since he had enlisted there, he had to use most of his savings again to get back to Durham when he left the Army.

There he joined the police force and met my mother. Their courtship helped the Roaring Twenties roar, and soon after they married an heir became apparent. Sure that I would be a boy, Dad practiced signing my name until he found one that looked and sounded good to him: "Joe Dennis Goodwin."

In the meantime, Dad was appointed to the new NC State Highway patrol. When he came to Watts Hospital to see me for the first time, he found a placard on my bassinet proclaiming me to be "Lt. Garland O. Goodwin, Jr." That which could not be denied was accepted, and I am now pleased to bear his name. However, when I started to school, I would rather have been just "Joe" and not had to explain and spell my name!

When the Patrol ordered standard motorcycles, the Harley folks sent my Dad a deluxe model, compliments of the company. I loved to sit with him on that big Harley and to hear its throaty roar when he left for work. My Uncle Wallace told me that once when Dad was working the State Fair, it included some stunt riders who put on quite a show on their motorcycles. Dad mounted his Harley and astounded them by performing all of their tricks!

I remember his sitting on the porch calmly reading the newspaper during a thunderstorm that produced the only "ball lightning" I ever saw. He said that if the Lord were going to take him by lightning, it would have happened in the South China Sea. He was right; he was fatally injured in someone else's car a year later. He was barely 35 years old, and I was eight.

Dad had learned to fly airplanes at some point, so he could answer my questions about how they fly. I made a cardboard model airplane with movable control surfaces so I could bend them to produce the maneuvers I wanted as I put them through the motions of loops and rolls and so forth. We also went aloft with a barnstorming pilot for my first airplane ride. So you see, he started me on my way to becoming a pilot and a designer of airplanes.

I have lived more years than either of my parents, but my Dad certainly packed more adventure into his short life than I have in mine. I wish he had had more time to train me, and that I could have heard these stories from his lips instead of Mother's. My parents loved each other and my younger brother and me very much, and I am thankful for my good fortune. I am the only one left to tell their stories, and I consider it more of a privilege than a duty to do so.

Party Animal
July 2003

This month's suggested topic is "Entertainment at Home," which means to me that you throw a party at your own house. Yes-s-s !

As a youngster I was rather shy with strangers. I would not answer the phone because I did not know who might be calling. I did not like to make calls because I did not know who might answer. Working in a newspaper office and later at a grocery store, meeting the public as part of my job, I was soon using the phone naturally.

It was the same thing again years later when I had to use two-way radio to talk to airport control towers and flight service stations. My instructor assured me that most people had "mike fright," but I still wrote down my numbers etc on a card for my first try. There was no pain, and the people were friendly, so radio talk became natural, too.

I never went to any parties while growing up, and there were never any at anyone's house in our family. There were some social gatherings at school and squadron parties in the Air Force, but it was not until college that I learned about real parties. We started having class parties at the homes of classmates and friendly faculty members. I enjoyed them.

My wife enjoyed both giving and attending parties, and we did some of both with our church groups. Then I asked Fran whether we might throw a party for my colleagues at work. She was enthusiastic, since she had friends in the wives' club, so we set about planning a Saturday night open house.

Everybody came and the house overflowed with happy people eating, drinking, talking and laughing. They did not start to leave until after midnight. As the first ones were retrieving their coats, I suggested Garland's first rule for party-goers: "Leave early for best selection!" I still get a laugh with that line.

The last ones wandered out at about 2 a.m., and the coats actually came out even (but we did find an extra pair of shoes, retrieved by a guest on a later visit.) As we turned down the covers I asked Fran if she thought it was a good party, if our guests had had a good time. She just gave me that look that I see often as I bumble my way through life with a smart woman.

We have given many parties over the years since then; we designed our dream house for having large parties. The kitchen is huge, because we discovered that if you have 50 people in, there will be twenty in the main room, five in the den, and the rest in the kitchen. The trouble with a large party is that the host spends the first two hours greeting people and the last two telling them goodbye.

I have learned not to use those little plates at parties. I just live hand to mouth so the hostess won't know how many ham biscuits and cream puffs I ate. I also have to sample everything in order to assure her honestly that all of it is good. I always let the lovely young woman fill my punch cup to enjoy her company and her smile (and so I don't make a mess!)

My Fran was amazed that I never had a birthday party while growing up. So she and a friend both burned their hands trying to get 50 candles lit for me to blow out at the blowout they put together for me on that occasion. I had become a regular party animal by that time. If we had not given a party in a month or so, I would ask Fran if it were not about time to plan one.

Some of the engineers said that they did not want a party when they left, but we told them that attendance by the guest of honor was optional. We would have the party anyway, eat his cake, and even toast dear old so-and-so in absentia. I once chided Fran about scheduling OUR Christmas party on the prime Saturday of the season when folks might have somewhere else to go, and she retorted that "If I am having a party, they will come HERE!" She was right, as always. Party, anyone?

The Weekend
August 2003

Our editor is of the tender age that she still works all week and therefore has weekends. She has suggested Weekend Adventures for our topic this month. *Prime Times!* are reputed to be those times when the workweek is a thing of the past and we seniors are to be enjoying the prime of our lives, all week long, every week. So what do we know of weekends?

I have always been puzzled by the term, since Saturday is the END of the week and Sunday is the BEGINNING of a new one. I suppose that the TGIF syndrome is powerful in all working people, so that the end of the week is more meaningful than the beginning. Many probably consider Monday as the beginning of the week, anyway, since that is when it is back to the ol' grind.

When I first joined the ranks of the weekendless people, I came home from my daily foray into town to ask my wife what Holiday it was. Both the bank and the Post Office were closed! She told me that it was Saturday, as if that explained everything.

It did not take us long to learn to shop on weekdays, preferably the days when some stores offer senior discounts. We also eat signature entrées at lunch prices by entering as the lunch crowd is leaving the restaurants. The health gurus tell us that we should eat our big meal in the middle of the day, so we know that we are doing the right thing. Trouble is, after having a big bowl of popcorn for supper, I often opt for a big bowl of ice cream at bedtime!

What constitutes an adventure for a senior citizen? The definitions of adventure include these words: hazardous, questionable, unusual, exciting, and risk. Unlike my Dad, I have not had many adventures, and I am not sure how much adventure I can handle now. Friend Barbara Grooman seems to have "MsAdventures" all the time, and appears none the worse for them. But then, she customarily makes lemonade from her lemons.

Do we have too much of the "been there, done that" syndrome to invite further adventure into our lives? Do some of those words that describe adventure put us off? I suppose I am now too chicken for "hazardous" and "risk." I don't do extension ladders any more, for instance. But I might have to look into something said to be "risqué!" (OK, I know that's not the same thing. But it might be!)

I am not sure about "questionable." Depends on who is questioning. If it is I, then I might decide to try it. If it is the wife, friends, or the law, then it's "No way, José!" Longevity is a part of my recipe for happiness. So is "peace on earth, goodwill toward men," as the carolers paraphrase Dr. Luke.

"Unusual" and "exciting" sound promising. Maybe there is yet opportunity for adventure for us even if we are not quite of the Indiana Jones or Xena the Warrior Princess mold. I like the Indiana Jones character, played so well by Harrison Ford, and I really did identify with his character that rebuilt that wrecked seaplane and got it airborne just in time to save his and the pretty lady's skins. I liked the pretty lady, too, especially when she let him get that water snake out of her britches. Now, that's adventure!

Not being a sports fan (I never did understand which end of a ball to hold to), it would be unusual for me to go to a ball game or a horse race. When I have done so, just to be sociable mind you, I found them exciting. Watching a major golf tournament on TV while away on a trip with a sports nut, I got to see Tom Watson blast out of a sand trap right into the hole. Another time, during a three-hole tie breaker, I saw both Tiger Woods and his equal of the day, each trying to get his ball from a ROAD back onto the course. So doing the unusual is a good way to add a little excitement to the mix of life.

Accept that invitation from a friend to do something you don't do every day. You will probably be delighted by a new (to you) dish at a restaurant, new music, a new acquaintance, a new appreciation of something you'd never really noticed before. Go for it! And just think, you don't have to wait for the weekend.

For Love of Books
September 2003

Our house is full of books. Aunt Mildred's house is full of books. At 86, she has pretty well stopped buying them, but at only 73, I just can't quit. I think they are more addictive than cigarettes and ice cream.

Our books cover a wide range of subject matter, much like a public library. They are arranged by category on our shelves: airplanes here, music there, biographies over there, and so on. We even have a separate bookcase for autographed books!

At first, we left spaces in the shelves for other stuff like *objets d'art* (we really don't have any of those, unless the piano player made from horseshoe nails qualifies) as suggested by our interior designer daughter. The den shelving looked real pretty for the first year or so, what with the hunter green wall behind (also her suggestion), but guess what? The new books have crowded the objects and some books are even lying flat on top of the vertical books or in front of them. Alas, the green wall is hardly visible.

Do we put books into the Friends of the Library sale? Of course not! We go there to get more. Friend Jim volunteered with the Friends in his city when he retired. His house is full of books, too, but now he gets first choice of the ones people bring in! And good friend that he is, Jim brings choice books to us when he comes to visit.

We like to travel together, too. We usually find our way around the country in terms of restaurants, but Jim is always on the lookout for little stores that offer used books. His primary quest is for additions to his collection of hymnbooks, but all books are of interest. One day his collection will have a place in some worthy institution of higher learning. I suppose my "collection" will be distributed by the Friends of the Library.

Most of us want to own our books so that we can go back to them from time to time for their content. Some of us like the look and feel of fine books and thus enjoy them without regard to content. Jim's intense love of books led him to learn the bookbinder's craft over at the Campbell Folk School in Brasstown. He repaired my Bible for me gratis while perfecting his skills. Every book lover should have such a friend! It is a wonderful thing to see a fine volume become beautiful and useful again as Jim patiently undoes unwitting damage and restores bindings, end papers, pages, and stitching as necessary.

My time is so taken by my volunteer activities that I manage to read only three or four books a year. If I could only remember to take one with me when I know I am going to sit in a waiting room, perhaps I could read two more. One trouble is that I like to read slowly, speaking the dialogue to myself in the appropriate cadence and accent. I also savor descriptions and the writer's use of language. Another trouble is that I can read for only about an hour and a half before my eyes say "Enough!" But at least I can still read.

Many of our friends either cannot see well enough to read, or can read only with great difficulty. The ones with macular degeneration have devices that put greatly enlarged images on a TV screen. At 95 years, my high school English teacher can see only one short word at a time on her screen. When she moved into a care facility she liquidated her library. I helped a bit by reading titles to her and then putting the books into stacks as directed. She was being very practical about something that must have grieved her, for I know that each book was a lifetime friend. And each friend was going to her friend who would cherish it most.

Rejoice if you can still see to read! Then go over and read to your friend who cannot. You'll both be glad you did.

Winterizing
Ants & Grasshoppers
October 2003

The coming of winter separates the ants from the grasshoppers, right? When the leaves take on all those pretty colors they trigger our ant instincts. That means we must do some things before the snows come. The grasshopper-types among us enjoy the beauty and enjoy the snow and then pay the man to fix the frozen pipes etc.

I suppose I am more ant than grasshopper because I do remember to take certain precautions. I disconnect the garden hoses, drain them and roll them up, but I don't put them in the garage yet because I might need them again. The leaves then cover them over so I cannot find them anyway. But when I dig them out in spring at least they are not split from having frozen.

The car gets a pretty good going over, as does the house. The lawn mower is supposed to be winterized after the last time the grass is mowed. You know the drill: drain the tank and run all the gas out of the carb, change the oil and sharpen the blade so it will be ready to go when you need it next spring. But how do you know which mowing is the last one? Around here the grass sometimes grows a-plenty in October. Would we then mess up our nice winterized mower to cut it one more time? No, better not waste a good winterizing by having to do it again. And since it is too cold to fool with a lawn mower in winter, I always winterized the thing in the spring. Now I let a young man mow the yard on a regular basis. I wonder if I winterized my lawnmower the last year that I used it? Probably not.

We made our master closets in our dream house big enough to house all of our clothes. In all of our previous houses we had to move clothes to and from other storage areas with the change of seasons. My wife has a rule for these closets, though: when I buy a new shirt an old one has to go to the thrift store. Good idea, for the replacement was not necessarily triggered by my outgrowing an older one. Same goes for pants, except that I have usually outgrown them. (Actually, it is all that washing and drying that makes them too small.)

Winterizing used to be a lot bigger deal, it seems to me. While growing up on a farm, I was outdoors a lot more than I am now, and for longer periods. That meant a heavy jacket and warm gloves, heavy boots and wool socks, and something to go on my head that would also keep my ears warm. Wood had to be stockpiled for both the cookstove and the fireplaces. The barn loft had to be filled with hay and fodder. And the ladies had to can and preserve as much food as possible to see us through the winter. There were no grasshoppers among the farm population, for only the ants survived.

We have a woodburning fireplace in our house, but the Peterson gas logs went in the same time the gas meter did. We also cook on a gas cooktop, so there are now no sawing, splitting and stacking of wood; just turn the little handle and pay the gas bill. Same goes for the cow and the mule that we don't have; no barn, no hay, no fodder. One thing we still do, though: We buy peaches in summer and freeze them so we can have cobbler and ice cream in winter.

I think I have been very fortunate to morph somewhat from an ant into a grasshopper. I spent far more years as an ant than I will get to enjoy as a grasshopper. But I am somewhat winterized, even if the mower is not, so I expect not only to survive, but to enjoy! Peach cobbler, anyone?

Food and Recipes
November 2003

Our editor has provided another opportunity for me to address a topic about which I am ignorant but enthusiastic. Eating can be one of life's great pleasures, and can still be enjoyed when other pleasures become unattainable. But before food can be eaten, it must be produced and prepared. Before one can enjoy, another must work. Many others, in fact.

I grew up on a farm so I know about food production firsthand. I milked the cow, fed the stupid chickens and gathered their eggs, hoed the weeds out of rows of vegetables, and was a fascinated but reluctant attendant at hog-killing time. I also learned about pack-saddle caterpillars while pulling fodder after having pulled the roastin' ears off the corn stalks some weeks earlier.

Yes, stupid chickens. I would put fresh mash in their trays and fresh water into their pan, kept full by an inverted mason jar. They would eat mash, drink water, eat more mash, and return for more water that now had mash floating on it from their beaks. They would look at me and not drink the now-contaminated water. They seemed to be imploring me to give them more clean water. Never happened. There is more evidence of their stupidity that I will not offer here.

Years later I plowed up our back yard in the city so I could raise vegetables. I rediscovered how much more flavorful fresh veggies are. The garden kept expanding until I had cucumbers growing on the chain link fence so I could use their former bed for cantaloupes. Even made room for watermelons one year! We learned years later that our daughter had thought we were poor because her clothes and bread were homemade and we grew our own vegetables.

So you see I know where food comes from and how to put it away. For many years I ate only the familiar things we had grown ourselves. Unlike our son, who as a teenager would eat anything that did not eat him first, I would not try new things. Then travel, wife and other new friends introduced me to many delightful flavors and foods. One friend attributed our being overweight to too much "recreational dining." Some of us used to eat to live; now we live to eat!

It is in the preparation of meals that I must admit to almost total ignorance. Of course I can make a peanut butter sandwich, but I can also fry eggs and bacon to perfection. Beyond that, I falter and do something like setting the table, slicing the bread or putting ice in the glasses. I can also cram all the stuff into the dishwasher when it's over.

Our local Kiwanis club sponsors a cooking class primarily for bachelors and widowers. About twelve guys go to the Extension office once a week where the Consumer Educator tries to turn them into chefs in a few easy lessons. We learned about the food groups and had homework. We practiced doing dry and liquid measures, peeling stuff, slicing and dicing stuff, mixing stuff and cooking stuff. The written instructions are called recipes, and we learned new meanings for words like combine, fold and blanch. Then we set the table and dined on our results. Thanks to the Educator's careful oversight, no one died.

Graduation was held at a fine local restaurant, where their chef allowed us to gather in his kitchen and watch him prepare our lunch. Inspiring and delicious it was, and though now wiser in the ways of the kitchen, I still prefer to let him or his kind prepare my meals.

Wife Fran reads recipes. It is beyond me how she can determine by mere words whether something will be good to eat. If it has a dozen ingredients and takes three hours to prepare, she turns the page. She has a library of cookbooks as big as my collection of airplane books, but she still asks what I would like for supper. I have to try to think of something, because if I say "Oh, I dunno" or "Whatever," I will probably get to make myself a peanut butter sandwich.

Gifts from the Heart
December 2003

In thinking about this subject, I have decided that ALL gifts come from the heart. The very idea of giving is foreign to our intellects, but is an imperative of our hearts. Of course I don't mean the pump, but that part of our self that relates to others. Remember how Red Skelton would follow a poignant story with "Gets ya right in th' pump, don't it?" while touching his chest?

We say that a person who is generous and always giving has a big heart. Does it follow that a person with a "big brain" will not be generous? Oddly enough, it does not. But I do think that for most of us, giving is a learned response. A child naturally wants the biggest piece of candy, to go first or to get first choice. Fortunately, most of us outgrow that and begin to share willingly and to give because we want to.

At the drive-through teller window, our little daughter would ask for another piece of candy "for my brother," and she would give it to him when we got home. In the same situation, our little bit older son would ask for another piece "for my sister," but he would just have to eat it before we got home! If something were to be divided, I would have one split it and then let the other have first choice. By the time they started to school they were pretty fair and generous.

(In fairness, I must tell you that this son spent nearly all the money we had given him for his vacation with his grandparents on a model of the MG sports car to give to ME!)

I had to learn to give. Since I was nearly four years old when my brother came into our family, I was already pretty well established as the center of my universe. Everybody paid attention to me and gave me things. I thought my toys were for my use exclusively, and I did not like it when little guests played rough with my cars and trucks and banged them up.

Little brother suddenly got nearly all of my mother's attention, and everyone who came wanted to see "the BABY." Some people would play with me or talk to me later, but it just was not the same. Why would I want to share anything with HIM? He wouldn't know what to do with it anyway!

When we begin to appreciate other people and form attachments to them, we then WANT to share with them and give to them. Many people do this naturally. They are the ones who arrive at your house with something when you have suffered the loss of a loved one, and pitch right in to make your other guests comfortable. They do not just tell you how sorry they are and add "If you need anything, just let me know" as they walk away.

My wife Fran is one of those people who is always giving, and she knows what to give. I want to give, but I never know what. For instance, shortly after Van Cliburn won the Tchaikovsky competition, I found his recording of the Concerto on the music rack of my piano before I even knew the thing had become available. She has done this sort of thing countless times in the years we have been married. She makes or buys perfect gifts all during the year for nearly everyone she knows.

On the other hand, if I think of something she'd like, I cannot remember what it was long enough to buy it. Sometimes I get it right, but more often I just take her out to dinner and hope for the best. At least I can make her a birthday or anniversary card the night before with my computer! This is not funny. I would like to do better, but I simply cannot. And I am afraid I am not alone in this failing.

However, the best gifts are not the ones from the store, but what we give of ourselves. Time is precious to all of us. We all have the same amount each day, so when we give our time to another it has value far beyond our "hourly rate." Just listening can be priceless.

As I wrote at the top, I think all giving comes from the heart. But some of us must learn to heed our hearts, while others are tuned in to them from the beginning. I wish I were one of those. Yes, I have given much, but I have received much more. We don't give to get, but somehow our gifts return to us in wonderful and surprising ways. Try it; you'll like it!

Retirement Living
The Flexible Retiree
January 2004

I retired some 15 years ago, and I am still alive, so I suppose I am qualified to address our editor's suggested subject this month. She gave us a lot of leeway, in that she lists nine subheadings as possibilities. Surely I will be able to hit on one or two of them, though some do not appeal to me because they contain words like Exercise, Jobs, Changes, and Aging. If you have read anything I have written before, you know that I don't do serious, and those things sound serious. The other writers can take care of those things.

I mean, I know that I need to get more exercise and make some "healthy changes" in my lifestyle. But these needs help me to be more like my peers and less of an oddball. When all of the others ask for a beer or a Coke, I order a Dr. Pepper. They are all driving SUVs or big pickups and I am just trying to stay out of their way in my nimble little Saturn. While they are watching Survivors or HGTV, I am channel surfing, or having a snack. While they are doing the Internet or solitaire, I am writing columns or editing old family photographs. But like every last one of our species, I am aging.

Well, maybe not. My mother said that when I was three years old, I would carry on intelligent conversations with adults. By the time I was nine I was too silly to talk to anybody. My wife Fran says that I am younger since I retired than I was before, so you see I am not even aging normally, let alone "gracefully" (another of our editor's suggestions).

As I said, I don't do serious, and I can't do graceful. Our daughter Sharon is a natural-born ballerina, but she is adopted. Fran says that dancing with me is like being paired with a Mack truck. But I can manage, because when I did the obligatory turn on the dance floor with Sharon at her wedding, I did not step on either of her feet. Nor her mother's, her mother-in-law's, nor her college friend's. The latter was great with child, which did tend to put her feet out of harm's way.

Now that I have written about the things I said I would not, I realize that even that matches my retirement experience. I never expected to be writing columns and magazine articles, though my half-dozen English teachers all told me that I should write professionally. I never expected to be president of our county Historical Association, since History was undoubtedly my worst subject in high school. The above, and being active in my Lions Club, got me into the Second Wind Hall of Fame, an organization after my own heart: we only meet once a year, and we have a nice luncheon.

I did expect to play my piano a lot, build stuff in my woodworking shop, and travel when I retired. None of those things have come to pass. Instead of "poor planning," I prefer to call it "flexibility." Most of our travel is to visit family somewhere, but Fran reads the AAA booklets to me as we ride along, so we sometimes make unscheduled stops. Travel is indeed broadening, because we sit in those bucket seats in our car and eat in great restaurants three times a day.

I know that we were expected to pick one and write all about it, but I think I have somehow managed to address all but two of her topics! I will take care of them now: I think my retirement is "meaningful," and I plan to "spend the winter" inside.

What's Good for the Heart
February 2004

Most of our editor's suggestions for this month are much too serious and important for me to risk misleading someone with my observations. This is also Heart Month. Perhaps my thoughts on that won't be life-threatening, if not taken seriously. You have been warned.

Some menus have little red valentines by certain entrées that the Chef contends are "heart healthy." DO NOT order any of that stuff if you enjoy eating. Chances are it will not have any butter in it, or anything else that would make it taste good and be easy to eat. No, you will struggle with barely steamed veggies, baked meat that cried out to be fried, and salads with no oil to help them slide easily down the little red lane.

Instead, you will encounter "interesting" flavors from so-called "herbs and spices" that you never heard of that attempt to make the stuff palatable. Sometimes it works, though, and the Chef must be commended for a really tasty dish. But don't count on it.

I grew up on good Southern cooking. That means that the green beans were cooked long in a big pot with a slab of fatback thrown in for seasoning. Same for turnip greens (no one in their right mind eats spinach, Popeye notwithstanding. Even as a kid I figured out that it was just a ploy.)

Corn could be fried (delicious!) or served as pudding, or just cooked. But when served on the cob (merely boiled in water, and presumably "heart healthy") it was promptly laced with butter, which melted into it right away, and made it very good eating. Potatoes are proof that God loves poor people, because they are delicious no matter how they are prepared. At our house a big chunk of butter always goes into the mashed or baked potatoes; the baked ones also get sour cream.

And speaking of cream, I generally add a dollop to my coffee to knock the edge off the taste. Real coffee lovers drink it straight, so I guess that lets me out. (Did you ever look at what is in that white stuff some people put in their coffee? Is THAT heart healthy? Heaven help us!) How about ice cream? Whenever we go up to Hendersonville of an afternoon the car naturally pulls in at Piggy's for a cone. I see a lot of healthy looking people there, so I keep going back.

As Emeril would say, let's kick those bran muffins up a notch by putting a dab of cream cheese on each bite. Better than butter! The ultimate combination for me is a sandwich made of date-nut loaf slices with a slab of cream cheese between, each item being at least a quarter-inch thick. Yum-m-m!

Getting back to potatoes, my wife Fran observes that I use French Fries to shovel ketchup into my mouth. I thought I learned that the tomato is a fruit, but the USDA says ketchup is a vegetable for school lunch purposes. Since both are on a good diet, does it matter which I am shoveling? I am getting my fruit/vegetable ration with an edible spoon!

Does chicken taste better any way other than properly fried? Does anything go better with eggs than market-sliced bacon cooked on the griddle (NOT microwaved—ugh!)? Would anyone want to eat a lobster tail without drawn butter and lemon juice? And of course I want "fries with that." Biggie? Why not! Some folks try to tell me why not, but I don't want to hear it. At my age, I have seen food that was good be called bad, to be followed in a few years by a switch back to good. I have already lived longer than many of my schoolmates, even my ancestors, so why should I have my cholesterol checked? I agree with Fran, who observes as she turns the bacon over, "We are not going to get out of this world alive anyway, so why not enjoy it while we are here?"

Computer for Fun & Profit
March 2004

The home computer has become as commonplace as radio, TV and music players. The first computers were single-purpose machines built to solve one complex mathematical problem, and had to be redesigned to solve the next one. Some filled rooms, others entire buildings. Then programming made the machines attractive to universities and industry, and integrated circuits made them small enough to carry around. Though they are still essentially "number-crunchers," most users of home computers are unaware that there is any arithmetic or geometry involved in what they do.

Now that computer hardware includes enormous storage capacity, printers, scanners and sound systems, plus software (the "programs" that tell the computer what to do) for every conceivable task, about the only thing your home computer cannot do is manual labor. But if you can come up with a machine to do that, the computer will operate it for you!

My wife Fran built our first computer from a kit in the late 70s. The whole thing was contained in the keyboard (see photo next page). We used an old black and white TV for its monitor, and I bought a little tape recorder to record and playback "programs." There was no printer interface yet, so there is a pad and pen to write down the answers. That little computer would do rudimentary calculations, but had to be programmed by the operator to do anything at all! It was really just a plaything demonstrating new technology.

I bought newer ones as they became more useful, and soon I was doing real work on them and printing out the results. The professional ones at work were fast, but the software was not "user friendly." By the time I retired I felt that I could justify owning a "real" computer to help me fulfill my engineering design contracts. Later, inkjet printers and scanners were

added to make up a very useful package indeed. For

me the home computer had arrived and was fulfilling its destiny.

At first Fran did not care whether we had a computer or not. She sends a LOT of greeting cards for all occasions and sentiments, so when I got a bigger computer, I also got her a greeting card program. Now she could create the many cards she wanted to send, and personalize them. We were on our way!

Soon we were both using the computer so much that when I needed an upgrade I bought a complete state-of-the-art system and passed my old one down to her. She opened a needlework shop and we did all the business printing in our computers: business cards, letterheads, order blanks, gift certificates, ads and all the signs for pricing and categorizing the stock. Meantime, I was producing several newsletters, signs and posters for the organizations I was part of. I was writing newspaper columns and magazine articles as well, and finally realized that e-mail would help us both.

We could not do half of what we do now without our computers. The Internet and e-mail are indispensable, and when a computer or our server goes down we are in big trouble. E-mail has cut our postage and long distance bills drastically, enough to more than pay for the service. My columns and articles are e-mailed to the publishers. We are in touch with friends all over the country on a regular basis that we used to hear from only at Christmas. The best part is you write at your leisure and they read at theirs; you don't have to be present at the same time as with the telephone. And it is in print, so it is easy to make a hard copy if desired.

Another addition to my computer activity is a digital camera. Now we can photograph something and have it in a newsletter or on a flyer coming out of the printer in a matter of minutes. Or we can e-mail a picture immediately to anyone interested. Photo editing is another valuable ability; I can take the glare off eyeglasses, get rid of red-eye in flash photos of people, and heal creases in (and white areas gouged out of) old family photographs. I even took the beard off an ancestor to see who now looks like him! I also produce a calendar for our extended family every year that has all the birthdays identified by red numbers, together with photos of each month's celebrants.

Computers are not for everyone, and many seniors have refused to even consider them. However, if you would like to do any of the things I have mentioned, you might want to learn about computers. A friend who teaches computer classes at her church has found it necessary to offer advanced classes as well as her introductory one because her students soon want to do more things. One lady started with her at age 91, and recently bought her second computer at age 96!

Lawn, Garden and Patio
A Place in the Yard
April 2004

When our children were starting to school we lived on an ideal city lot. It was on a banjo (you probably understand *cul-de-sac,* but from the air the dead-end street with turn-around looks like a banjo to this farm-boy pilot), so the front yard was small and the back yard was big.

A very short street frontage means there is not much yard in public view. A front yard is similar to the parlor of a farm house; it is only for show and has no other use. Just as we didn't go into the parlor unless we seated company there, we go into the front yard only to pretty it up for passersby. If you like growing ornamentals and caring for shrubs and grass, fine. Enjoy! I will smile in appreciation as I go by yours, but I am happier when I can hire someone to take care of mine.

Over the years, I traveled back to my home place periodically to visit, and enjoyed fine meals from the gardens of family and friends. Then I just I had to have my back yard plowed up for a garden. It was fun at first, and the good vegetables were certainly worth it, but soon there was no time to sit on the patio and enjoy watching the veggies and melons grow. They all require periodic encouragement, like weeding and watering, digging up and re-planting, and other sweat-inducing activity. Most of them like summer best, but I like air-conditioning best.

We combined the swing sets etc with our next-door neighbor and soon most of the kids on our banjo were playing in our bigger back yards. We decided that they should also have sand to play in, so we ordered a yard of sand from a building supply place. Or maybe it was a ton; anyway, that is NOT the way to buy sand to play in. It duly arrived, in a little pivoted bucket on the back corner of a huge lumber truck. The driver backed to where we wanted the sand, pulled a little lever, the bucket tipped, the sand ran out, and the bucket flipped back into its latch in its original position. It was all over in two seconds, and as the driver left we noticed how tiny the pile of sand was.

No matter; all the kids converged on it and soon it was spread out on an area about the size of a throw rug. Still, it looked like a beach, so they all went to put on their swimsuits. What is a beach without water? One of them pulled the hose over to the beach and doused everyone thoroughly, with much squealing and laughter. Our sand pile was obviously a hit!

That lasted all of five minutes before they decided to do something else. They disappeared suddenly, leaving the hose running to wash the beach into the nearby storm drain. So much for that.

Ever notice how eager a boy is to run the lawn mower when the handle is above his head, but by the time his waist comes up to the handle, his hands somehow cannot find it? I guess I never outgrew that notion myself, for I was secretly glad when we moved across town to a bigger house with tiny yards all around, and so many trees that nothing much would grow around it.

Yes, a good yard has several functions. It must make the house look good from the street. If you love to drive the riding mower, then a three-acre sweep of lawn up to your door is for you; it will consume your whole Saturday morning. Every one of them. If you have a green thumb, then almost any yard will provide many opportunities for showing off your skills. If no yard at all, how about window boxes?

The yard should also provide play areas for the kids, perhaps a putting green for Dad. DO NOT mount the basketball hoop on a wall of the house. Our house shook almost continually, even into the night. When we built a detached garage and moved the hoop there, I had to put protective slats over the windows in its big door. Be careful to what you allot space in your yard!

Like anything else, a good yard requires thought and action. It can be a joy or something else, according to how much of the preceding its owner wishes to give it. Condo, anyone?

Home Interiors Primer for Men
May 2004

I have already written about Home Décor (p.24). While this subject almost never comes up in the conversations of real men, it is one that apparently never *stops* coming up among women. This is written for men, but women might also find it helpful. These topics were suggested by our editor.

(1) Accessories: Men want a big comfortable chair, a big comfortable bed, a big color TV, a place to eat where they can see the TV, and a bath with a shower. Everything else in the house is accessories, and these are best left to the women. I mean, why should the husband have an opinion about the color or kind, or whether to get drapes or blinds?

(2) Painting: See above. But if you cannot avoid becoming involved, try to hire a professional. He/she will get in and out before you can get enough stuff together to start the job. The paint will be applied only to the surfaces the wife wants painted, and your foursome won't have to replace you.

(3) Furniture: If there are children or animals, get the furniture from Goodwill, so that it already looks like new furniture will look after the first week. Use the savings to get a bigger TV.

(4) Hardwood floors: These are beautiful unless you walk on them, or put furniture on them. Better cover them with carpet or vinyl right away, so the next owner can rip off the protection and enjoy caring for a still-beautiful floor. I learned this in the 50s when everyone immediately put covers on the seats of a new car, and kept them covered until the car was sold. Then the buyer would have a five-year-old car with new seats.

(5) Mattress: Let her choose the bedstead, but insist on trying out the mattress yourself while she does so. Remember, you will spend about a third of your life on it, so choose it well. And don't worry, she will awaken you when it is time to sign the papers.

(6) Decorating the Family Room: See (1); note that (3) is especially true here.

(7) Styles in furniture. Most new furniture comes in groupings, sometimes called "suites," that are similar in appearance. Women especially like this attribute, and it might be difficult to achieve at the Goodwill store. There are some decorators, however, who are adept at the mix-and-match game. You might want to become involved enough to steer her toward one of them, so you get to keep some of what you have. You realize, of course, that the rest will go to Goodwill to keep the cycle going.

(8) Decorating your windows. The first word is key here; see (1).

(9) Installing wallpaper. Do you realize that wallpaper costs a great deal more than the wall it is stuck to? And that if the wall is already papered, you should consider it permanent? Do not believe the DIY pamphlets they give you at the store that show and tell you how EASY it is to remove and hang wallpaper! Unless the wall was properly prepared for the paper, some of the wall is going to come off with the paper. What you have then is a wall that cannot be either painted or papered until something is done about the damage. Again, do your utmost to avoid becoming involved in any way with wallpaper! See (2) above. PLEASE!

I offer the above to you as a friend with a lot of experience with houses both new and old, in nearly every part of our great country. I designed and built with my own hands our present house, and have done all of the jobs associated with building and maintaining a house. We have furnishings from the store (both new and antique), from Goodwill, and from my workshop. So I am serious when I recommend that unless you really enjoy these tasks (and opportunities!) because you are good at them, call a pro and then relax and enjoy their handiwork. Either way, let your house truly be your home, where you and those you love live happily ever after.

Ode to our Personal Services People
June 2004

Most of us depend on other people who are willing to help us look good and stay healthy. Since they work on our person, not the car or the house, we place great importance on their ability and reliability. We choose them carefully and hope they and we will live happily ever after.

For the first half of my life I got my hair cut at the barbershop by a man. Then some of my friends told me that I should go to Nancy. My wife Fran liked the way their hair looked, and my male barber always complained about having to cut a "flat top" on my pointy head, so it was agreed that I should see Nancy. Nancy made the best of the situation, as I wanted to let my hair grow out so it could be combed and "styled."

Soon she had me looking great (well, my hair, anyway) and I learned that she was a really good softball player. Nancy always seemed to be glad to see me, and I was certainly happy to sit in her chair for a little while and swap stories. But after several years, Nancy moved away, and I had to find another barber/hair stylist. Whatever.

With my sparse, thin, straight hair and misshapen head, I present a challenge to any hair practitioner. When I went in again, there was a new girl sitting in Nancy's chair, and she stood as I approached and invited me to sit. That did not work out well, and I tried others, but none could do for my hair what Nancy did. They were not as interested in me, either; for them, I was just another head to be sheared. No stories.

For many years after Nancy, few of the barbers cut my hair to suit Fran. I would let it grow pretty long between visits, so I would always caution the barber to find my ears before he started cutting. Then one day I entered a hair styling salon to ask about putting a poster in their window. The lady I talked to seemed friendly enough, but she was looking mostly at my hair. When I turned to go to the window with my poster, she observed that "You need a haircut."

I agreed, but told her that I had really bad hair and most people did not want to try to work with it. With that, she told me to sit in her chair. She ran her comb through my hair several times and then began to cut here and there with her scissors, finally parting and combing my hair. I thought it looked good. Fran thought so, too, so now Doris takes care of both of us. Happiness is indeed finding the right hair care person!

The same is true for our health care persons. I have known our dentist most of his life, and we always talk about our MGs. I marvel that another person in his office is willing to scrape and polish my teeth periodically. Her work reminds me of the little bird that cleans the alligator's teeth without fear of being swallowed. Thanks to their efforts, I still have most of my own teeth.

Many other members of the medical profession stand ready to help when needed, and sometimes they become friends as well. When we have needed surgery there has always been a friend (or a friend of a friend!) available to do the cutting. Actually, I was more concerned with the anesthetists; anyone can "put me to sleep," but I am intensely interested in ascertaining whether I am likely to wake up! So far, we have recovered nicely.

When a visiting friend from another state needed emergency surgery, the hospital staff asked who we wanted to do it. The friends looked at us, and in unison we named "my" surgeon. They all smiled broadly and assured us that we had made an excellent choice. Friend's wife almost stopped worrying!

I wrote about the ophthalmologist who performed my cataract surgery ("Piece of Cake," Jan. 2001 *Prime Times!)* because I am so thankful that he learned the procedure and was willing to perform it for me. I now see 20/20 without glasses and have my very first unrestricted driver's license! Dr. Perraut and his technical assistants are now good friends, and they are still checking my eyes regularly.

Our family doctor was a fellow engineer in Texas where he and I owned an airplane together. Later he went to med school and opened his family practice in Spartanburg shortly before I retired. Since I do not want to find another doctor, I asked John one day whether he was thinking about retiring. He looked a little puzzled and replied in the negative. I told him that he had just made my day.

John and I always have to swap a few flying stories when I come into his office. One day he showed me a photo of the high-performance sailplane he had just bought. Aha! I was immediately reassured that my friend and physician will remain in practice. As long as he is still buying expensive toys, he will have to keep working, right?

I feel richly blessed to have so many friends who take such good care of me. I cannot say that everything they do to me is FUN (Doris takes a fiendish delight in spraying cold water on my hair before she cuts it!) but I am grateful for every one of them. May God richly bless them even as they have blessed me.

The Veteran
July 2004

To live in the United States is a blessing beyond measure. Who gave us this blessing?

The founding fathers risked their lives (and many later lost everything, including their lives!) to put down on paper the ideals that produced our nation. Even they were a vocal minority in a growing country made up of people who had never had it so good in spite of the hardships they faced in taming a wilderness. The politicians could declare independence, but they had to get enough ordinary people excited about it to achieve it.

The men who answered the call to arms and the women who supported them won the freedoms we enjoy today. Their successors have continued the fight when necessary, and it is these people we now call "veterans" that we celebrate and salute because we appreciate what they have done for us.

My family has answered the call many times during my lifetime. Uncle Ethan, brother Bill and cousin Earl were Marines; uncle Wallace, brother-in-law Terry, and cousin Linwood served in the Navy; father Garland Sr., father-in-law Bob and brother-in-law Mitch served in the Army; cousin Bryant flew B-29s for the Army and later B-36s for the Air Force, and my son and I served in the Air Force. We are thankful that all survived their wars and came home to enjoy the way of life they helped to preserve for us.

My first war was World War II. Everyone I have talked to remembers exactly where they were when they heard that the Japanese had attacked Pearl Harbor. Our country was struggling to come out of the Great Depression while the war clouds gathered in Europe and the Far East. Many hoped to avoid involvement overseas and our leaders had difficulty getting any preparations started for defending ourselves. Pearl Harbor united us and mobilized us to become involved in preserving our country from all enemies.

WWII was the last war that the whole country was committed to winning. Production of consumer goods was halted as the nation geared for total war. We had price controls and rationing. We made do with what we had and everything was recycled. It seemed that every family sent someone to war or to the defense plants. We barely won that one, but we accepted the unconditional surrender of the Axis nations, then set about rebuilding their countries as well as ours.

Many people who have dedicated their lives to defending our country have been called upon many times since then to go to war. The rest of the people were allowed to continue life as usual in a country devoted to prosperity and living the good life. For the veteran, this new kind of warfare is something like going out into a fierce thunderstorm to get more wood for the fireplace, then coming back inside to find that the family enjoying the cozy warmth did not even realize that he had gone out, let alone thank him for it.

Some have called these "unpopular wars." Some have resisted every war ever fought. But would we be an independent nation if we had not fought England? Would we still be "one nation" if we had not had the Civil War? Would we still be speaking English if we had not won both WWI and WWII? They were not "popular" either, but most have conceded that they were necessary.

The people who train hard to defend our country are too often put in harm's way for questionable reasons, in my opinion. But as the "old salts" used to say, "Ours is not to reason why, ours is but to do or die." They go where they are sent and do what they are told. Because of them, we do not have to do that.

The politicians are quick to send our "troops" to battle drug lords, warlords, dictators, whatever. Would that they would be as quick to pass bills that would lift the troops' pay above qualifying for food stamps, build and staff enough VA hospitals to treat their war-related ills, and elevate their status to at least "valued citizen." The way disabled vets have to struggle just to live suggests to me that the ones resting under the rows of white crosses are the lucky ones.

We remember them on Memorial Day, but what about the ones who survived minus important body parts and with permanent mental and physical disabilities? I think we should remember them, too, by including their timely care and postwar rehabilitation in the high cost of making war. Since we acknowledge our great debt to the veterans, why don't we give them their due? Maybe it's because they don't send us a bill.

Groceries in My Lifetime
August 2004

This month we address changes in something that have taken place during our lifetime. We all need groceries, whether we grow them or buy them. We all eat as regularly as we can, too, whether at home or at the cook's place. During my lifetime, I have obtained my edibles in all of these ways. That is why I have chosen groceries, a topic of universal interest.

I was born in Durham NC and lived a good portion of my first decade there. Mother bought most of our groceries at the A&P store, but she sent me to a little neighborhood grocery for a loaf of bread between times. I well remember the cry that went up in the land when the price of a loaf of bread went from a dime to 11 cents in 1939.

Another source was a mule-drawn wagon that came down our street every afternoon. It was laden with fruits, vegetables and things like watermelons and cantaloupes in season, all harvested that morning. The wagon had a thick canvas "roof" and a spring scale swung from a beam at the rear corner. Some things were sold by each, others by the scoop, still others by the pound. You brought your own basket out to carry your selections back into the house.

My wife Fran was born in Hillsboro TX where her grandfather owned a neighborhood grocery store. It had a single gas pump out front and a small meat market in back. Granddaddy Earl (see photo) hand-pumped the gas up to a glass tank on top, then

cleaned your windshield while the gas drained down into your car. If you wanted chops, he would throw a carcass onto the butcher block and carve off exactly what you wanted. He would jot down the prices on a paper bag, add them up, collect your money, and then put your order into the bag.

As a young child, Fran (center in photo below) was allowed to sell some things to the school kids who stopped in. When caught eating one cookie

for each one she sold, she was then compelled to eat the rest of the box. Grandma Zoe (left in photo) was in tears as Granddaddy Earl (right) enforced the entire punishment, but the only lasting effect was that Fran did not eat one of those cookies again until long after her own kids had left the nest.

During my second decade we moved to Polk County NC and my Grandfather Rippy's small farm. Now I was big enough to work a garden and milk Mama Rippy's cow. I thus earned a half-gallon of sweet milk a day and all the buttermilk we wanted. In Durham, the milk arrived in quart bottles, placed on the doorstep before dawn. Now, I extracted the milk from its source before dawn, and carried a jar of it back home with me. It was still warm, of course, so we finished up yesterday's milk from the fridge at breakfast. We had also poured off some of the cream, after it came to the top, for Mother's coffee.

During High School, I worked afternoons in a small grocery store in Tryon. My boss had been the manager of the A&P store before he took over the little store when its owner went away to WWII. How did we compete with the big A&P with its lower prices and house brands? (I was grown before I realized that the Ann Page brand was derived from the store name.) Our customers could call in their order and pick it up later, or have it delivered to their kitchen door. Some would drop off their list and by the time they had finished their other errands in town, I had put their groceries into their car (cars were never locked in those days, and the keys were usually in the ignition switch.) Most customers had charge accounts and paid at the end of the month.

Many things were rationed during WWII, so there would be some for everyone. We had plenty of Hershey bars and Rinso (not rationed), but rather than put them on the shelves where people we had never seen before could snap them up, we added our customers' favorites to their orders when appropriate. That is when I learned the value of being a loyal customer as well as being an accommodating business owner.

Now the "neighborhood store" has a forest of gas pumps in front and a large selection of snacks and "fast foods" inside. You can "pay at the pump," fill your tank and clean the windshield yourself, and be on your way again without so much as a tip of the hat to the owner. Or you can go inside to the john, find something to eat or read, and tip your hat to the clerk as you pay. (The owner is probably in another state, or even another country!)

The self-serve grocery stores became supermarkets and grew further in recent years by adding a deli and bakery inside and a gas station outside. Milk now has little cream in it, and even that is homogenized, so you have to buy cream separately (and it is only half-and-half; I wonder what the other half is?) Everything is pre-packaged and marked with a barcode that is read by laser beams so the checkout clerk usually does not even have to punch any keys. The computer keeps track of inventory and tells the manager what you bought today as well as what he needs to order to keep his shelves full.

Many things have changed, but there are still people working in the mega-stores doing exactly what I did: stocking the shelves and keeping the floor clean.

How to Save Money
September 2004

For some at the extremes of society, this subject has no relevance. Some people have so much money coming in from their investment holdings that they could never spend it all anyway, so saving would just add to the pile and generate even more money that they could not manage to spend. Others can barely subsist on the money available to them, so any money that they did manage to save would soon have to go for absolute necessities.

But for those of us fortunate to have what the economists call "Disposable Income," or money left at the end of the month instead of month left at the end of the money, there are some considerations for what we might do with it. Most of us can make some choices in the disposition of our money.

I had a ceramic piggy bank when a small child. Some relatives put coins into my hand, but others made a show of putting them into my piggy bank. It did not matter much to me at first, because I had few opportunities to buy anything anyway. When I got bigger and went with Mother to Kress's or Woolworth, I found a lot more than candy to be of interest. And the money in my hand never seemed to go far enough, so I was learning that money had to be managed somehow. I had to decide between candy gone in an instant and a balsa glider that might last a week or more.

Still later, not being allowed to break the bank, my brother and I learned how to get money out of our pigs with the blade of a table knife. Shaking the bank was pretty futile, but we could maneuver the coins against the blade and deflect them to the outside while lying on our back, holding the pig on its back above us.

Just as Robert Fulghum wrote that he learned in kindergarten all he really needed to know, all of the essentials of money management are contained above: money can be spent or saved; even money saved can be spent. The choices we make about every dime determine what other choices we may have, both now and later on.

Both my employers and my banking institutions made saving very easy and convenient, so I took advantage of the opportunities provided. Just as my daughter is a born shopper, I am a born spender. Bigger and better (read more expensive) toys have always tempted me. Just as I set the cruise control on my car mainly to keep me from speeding (as well as rest the gas pedal foot), I signed up for savings plans to keep me from spending it all.

One problem for me was that the interest on savings often did not keep up with inflation, so that the more money I saved, the more I lost in buying power. And when we paid the income tax on the meager interest earned, we were actually losing money by trying to save it. We did not begin to get ahead financially until the advent of the 401K plans and employers matching some of the funds that we saved.

The key to financial success is to spend less than you make, and then to invest the difference wisely. Everyone knows that. Easier said than done. When I was small, my mother gave me an allowance. So when I went to work, I gave myself an allowance. I found that regardless of the amount I allowed myself, it was pretty well gone by the time for the next installment. So I gave myself a small allowance to curb my spending.

I have always had a low threshold for prying the coins out of the piggy bank. When that new toy costs X dollars and there is almost X dollars in the bank . . . mighty tempting! But a wise older engineer once told me that if you have the price of TWO of those toys in the bank, maybe you won't have to buy even one of them. He was right, because my smaller allowance let my savings grow enough that I could easily choose whether to buy that toy or fatten the piggy some more.

To sum up: to save money, don't spend it. To keep from spending it, don't put it in your pocket; leave it in the bank. That way, when opportunity knocks, you can welcome it and act on it if you wish. Or you can wait for a better one. Either way, it is YOU making the choice, not your pocketbook. And one more thing: when you have enough saved for TWO rainy days, spend some to do something you've always wanted to do while you still can. You've earned it, so enjoy!

Getting There
October 2004

A convention speaker I heard in 1975 based his presentation on how recently man has become able to travel faster than a horse can gallop. Of course I had not thought of that and was impressed by his graph (engineers LIKE graphs!) With time measured horizontally and speed vertically, his chart was simply a straight horizontal line until the present, then an almost vertical line to the velocity of the manned spacecraft then beginning to orbit the earth. The last century or so, when all of the change occurred, was so tiny on the time scale that the curve just turned north and went off the chart like the rocket it represented.

When I arrived in this world, the Model A Ford was taking a lot of people wherever they wanted to go, often without benefit of a prepared roadway. My Dad had to be able outrun them on his Harley, because that was part of his job as a charter member of the North Carolina Highway Patrol. When Henry started putting V-8 engines in his little Fords, then they could outrun just about everything on the roads. Trouble was, there were very few roads that permitted speeds much faster than a galloping horse!

As a boy, I enjoyed riding in the rumble seat of Uncle Pete's Model A Ford convertible. My own family used to take Sunday afternoon drives in Dad's

Pontiac sedan. I can remember lying in the back seat as a toddler, watching the tops of the telephone poles go by. In those days there were three or four horizontal beams atop each pole, each beam carrying perhaps eight wires looped through glass insulators. I was later quite surprised to see how large those insulators were!

As an individual, my means of travel was walking or running, same as a horse. My wheeled toys did not provide much speed, except going downhill, and did not go far off our premises. My first means of going faster than I could run was a used bicycle. It provided thrills as well as transportation. We used to build ramps to ride up and jump, sailing through the air for ten or fifteen feet. High adventure, indeed!

I was fifteen when I used my grandfather's 1935 Buick to get my first license to drive. The license did not give me access to vehicles, so my driving time was pretty limited at first. I did get to substitute on the grocery delivery truck when its regular driver was not available. I later gained experience driving a light truck for a lumber company for college money. Still not much speed, though!

I learned to fly airplanes the summer I was sixteen, but those little planes were not fast either. I did find that I could exceed a hundred miles per hour in a dive, but it was just a number on a dial. No telephone poles going by up there!

In the nearly sixty years since I made my first solo flight, I have enjoyed ever-decreasing times required to "get there." We now routinely cover more than "a mile a minute" on the Interstate highways, and today's airliners move us at speeds just a tad less than that of sound. Any of us with the price of a ticket can cross the oceans or our country in less than a day. The astronauts go "Around the World" in about 90 minutes instead of Verne's 80 days.

Is "Getting There" really half the fun, as the ads suggest? That depends. Many weary travelers who MUST get there many, many times would probably answer that with a look. The daily commute and airline security measures have taken a lot of the joy out of necessary travel. And don't we plan our errands to accomplish as much as possible in one trip?

Remember when it was FUN to drive a car? It not only beat walking, but also provided opportunities to master new skills and explore new territory. For me the airplane was a similar challenge. Later on I got a small sailboat, which was fun but not used for getting anywhere. There are a lot of horses being kept around here where I live, and I don't think they are used for getting there any more either. So perhaps not getting there at all can be all the fun one could wish for. A horse need not gallop nor a sailboat leave a white wake in order to provide a most satisfying afternoon.

We took our five-year-old granddaughter for a Sunday afternoon drive while she was visiting us here. She kept asking where we were going and when we would get there. We did visit a sheep farm and some other places, but the idea of just riding in a car without a destination made no sense to her. Her life is already so structured that she does not know how to enjoy just looking at the world and sky and seeing whatever it offers and whatever comes next.

There are times to mount your race horse and spur him to gallop, but there are times for the old gray mare too, don't you think?

A Traditional Christmas?
November 2004

A traditional Christmas depends on whose tradition it is, for there are as many ways to celebrate Christmas as there are people doing it. I have enjoyed being shown or told what people in other parts of the world do, for Christmas seems to bring out the best in all people—for a time, at least. A birth should always be a happy occasion, and the birth of the Savior is especially salutary for those prepared for His coming.

The common thread of all celebrations is feasting, and Christmas may well be the greatest of all. Our family has always enjoyed a big Christmas dinner, even during the Great Depression. We all gathered at my grandparents' house, where their small farm provided most of what was on the table. As the cousins grew up and married, the uncles and aunts became grandparents, so there were more gatherings at more places. My immediate family all moved to California, so we did not always make it to the family gatherings still held in these parts.

My wife Fran loves to cook, and the more diners the merrier. When our family was not big enough, we invited enough "strays" to extend the table and surround it completely. There would be the new hire at work whose family was still back where he came from, an Army or Navy kid who could not afford to go home, and maybe a single from church who might otherwise dine alone. This happened more often at Thanksgiving than at Christmas, because nearly everyone will manage somehow to be home for Christmas!

I think a traditional Christmas, then, means a feast with as many of family and friends as can be gathered, even if the feast and the gathering must move around the area to include all of them. But I must say that for me, some Christmases have not been traditional!

I had my first Christmas away from home at age 18. I was in the Air Force, going to school in Wyoming, and could not afford to go home. There were only a dozen or two of us left in the squadron when the Blizzard of the Century hit in 1948. We awoke to find the barracks so cold that the mercury was not showing in the thermostat and the water in the toilets had frozen and split the bowls. The lone airman on fireman duty had been unable to keep the barracks furnaces going, so we gathered in the only warm building: the mess hall. The cooks managed a breakfast, and then we were given our duty assignments.

Mine was to get the furnace going in my barracks. The First Sergeant had not ordered any coal in months because he wanted what remained in the bins to be burned first. The largest pieces of coal I could find in my bin were about the size of my thumb. The grate in the furnace was in several pieces, so I propped them up on bricks to make a bed for a fire. I went into the barracks to get paper and I got an apple crate at the mess hall. The blizzard was still going, and the wind was blowing about 60 mph with stronger gusts.

I would fill the shovel and hold it up to let the wind blow the dust away from the pieces that then went into my basket about ten feet away. Before I could light my layers of combustibles, another airman came by with a basket of coal that he had liberated from the dry cleaning office at the other end of the squadron area. So I trudged down there and filled my basket with baseball-sized pieces of coal, and soon had a roaring fire going in my furnace.

After being in bitter cold for more than an hour, everything hurt as I began to warm up. There I was,

2000 miles from home, alone in my little furnace room, at Christmas. The pain and loneliness overwhelmed me at that point and I just cried for a while. There was no one to see or care, so I just let it all go. But as I warmed up and the pain began to go away, I began to feel that this might be my best Christmas yet. Why? Because I had bought presents for everyone in my extended family that always gathered for Christmas, and I knew that those little presents were under my grandmother's tree.

Santa Claus
December 2004

Ten year-old boys overheard in the hallway between Sunday School and church: "Do you think the Devil is for real?" "Nah. He is like Santa Claus; it's your father."

And I'd bet that in a similar discussion about angels, he would say that they are our mothers. But if Santa Claus is not just a fat guy in a red suit trimmed in white fur, with a flowing beard to match, but is really the Spirit of Christmas, then both Mom and Dad have a part in making him real for their children.

What is the Spirit of Christmas? Inspired by having received the greatest possible Gift from God our Father (He GAVE his only begotten Son, remember? John 3:16) we want to give to others. Since

I think that is what Santa Claus is about, I am a firm believer that he is indeed real.

I see our role as parents as keeping ol' Santa real until the children make the transition from getting to giving and truly understand that it is "more blessed to give than to receive." Let them help to set out the plate of cookies and the glass of milk for Santa; it is a nice reward after you get those bicycles put together. Let them be a part of the conspiracy; they don't want us to find out that they know, either! They won't let on if you don't.

Help them to select gifts for their siblings (after all, they know what they really want) and later suggest that they use their own resources to make or buy presents. Encourage them to give outside their family as they get older. Some presents cannot be wrapped, either coming or going. Those are the best ones.

Another good present is to be together as family, at least to start the Day. Then it is good to get the extended family together, even if Granny is a busybody and Gramps is a grump. All this togetherness could heal old wounds and a merry feast might make it one big happy family again, at least for a day. Who knows, the good feelings might last longer than that!

Of course, duty and distance can make physical togetherness impossible. Then it is time to run up the phone bill by letting everybody talk. Send a bit of home to the ones far away so that they will have something to touch and feel—or eat! These gifts don't have to be expensive, just given.

And finally, don't let the Politically Correct media steal our celebration. Send Christmas cards to everyone, not Season's Greetings. Choose the ones with angels, shepherds, wise men and the star of Bethlehem, that also include the real Star, the Christ child. If we do not remind people that He is the Reason for the Season, who will? See this as an opportunity to send God's Good News to everyone you know. In view of what He has done for us, can we do less for Him?

Prime Times! did not publish a January 2005 issue.

Self Improvement?
February 2005

Our new editor obviously does not know me as yet, or he would realize that I cannot be improved. Lord knows, my dear wife has tried, indeed is still trying . . . but you may agree that some people are more trying than others.

Most of us think we don't need much improvement, while some of us are afraid that we are beyond help. Can we improve ourselves, or do we need outside help? One of the "changing a light bulb" jokes suggests that the light bulb must want to change. So any improvement must be self-inflicted, because we cannot be unscrewed like a light bulb.

Neither my loving wife nor my many patient teachers could open up an access panel on my noggin, make necessary adjustments or pour in knowledge, and close me back up again a better person. No, I have had to listen and try to learn. I took notes and practiced. I did my homework. I read books and manuals. The result has been a largely successful and happy life for me.

As we approached our 50th wedding anniversary, a long-time friend observed to me that Fran and I seem to have a good marriage. I told him, "It's all her fault . . . she can get along with anybody!" Another time, when she was enjoying an extended visit with her family in Texas, I commented to a friend here who asked where Fran was, that they should understand that "someone married to me must have some relief" now and then.

As with most attempts at humor, there is some underlying truth involved here. I am revealing that I realize that I am not a perfect husband, much as I would like to be. This light bulb does want to change, but it is a lot easier said than done. I think that a lot of what we are is built in. We can learn to be "good" but we really are "bad" (our Creator says so). Unless we work at being "good," we will revert to type and mess things up big time. So when our friends love us in spite of our faults, we must not even think the usual retort, "What faults?"

The doctors give us pills, but we will not get better if we do not take them. Our trainer gives us exercises, but we won't improve if we do not do them. Our teachers give us homework, but we won't learn much if we don't do it. Those who love us offer advice, but our relationships will not get better if we ignore it. So I think all personal improvement is self-improvement when it comes right down to it. People can offer help, but it is still up to us to act on it.

With the New Year hard upon us as I write this, I realize that it is time once again to think about improving ourselves. Will I make resolutions? Yes. Will I keep them? Well, for a while anyway. How about you?

Hobbies and Sports
March 2005

I have too many hobbies and I am not into sports as most men are. My father, his brother and my brother excelled at playing baseball. My adopted son was born a Cowboys fan and was a sports writer for a while. Biologically speaking, however, I probably *am* a sport: *An organism that shows a marked change from the normal type or parent stock, typically as a result of mutation.* How else to explain how I got this way?

Since the Super Bowl is a non-event for me, I missed the celebrated "wardrobe malfunction" last year. It was shown a hundred times on every TV outlet in the world, so I did happen to see it once. Well, almost. It happened so quickly that I almost missed it anyway. I think Janet is a winsome lass who probably cried all the way to the bank.

I worked on many projects with the same two other engineers, one of whom dubbed our happy trio the "Normal Brothers—Abby, Sub, and Not." I never asked which one I was, but we shared many good times and enjoyed many successes. Is not being "normal" OK? On reflection, I think that a lot of the people who left their mark on our world so that everyone knows their name, even centuries later, might not be considered "normal," either. So I don't feel sorry for myself.

Everyone should have at least one hobby. Otherwise, it is all work, or worse, boredom. I do feel sorry for anyone who claims to be bored, because I don't understand the concept. With so much to see and hear and wonder about, how can anyone be bored? When someone complains that there is "nothing to do," suggest a chore and see how quickly he/she finds something else to do!

Some writers suggest that a hobby may be ridden, thinking perhaps of a hobby horse. I did enjoy the ride in my airplanes and sports cars, but anything big enough to ride gets expensive. But then, so do cameras, computers (and the stuff that makes them useful), tools, pianos, music, books, travel, fine dining, and so on. I still enjoy all of the above, but since I have not found a way to enjoy some of them for free, I must enjoy less often than I might want.

But that is not a bad thing. Think about it. When you have just enjoyed a fine meal, complete with dessert, would you want to move immediately to another dining room where an equally fine feast awaited you? The rarity of some pleasures tends to intensify our enjoyment of them. So happier is the person who has something else to enjoy when he finishes a book or the concert ends.

Sometimes avocations turn into vocations. My piano playing definitely is not in the professional category, but in trying to get my own piano working right, I eventually became a professional piano technician. Now I get to meet many wonderful pianists as I service the pianos they play. And I feel that being a wannabe pianist myself, I can better understand and produce the results the artists want.

One thing is certain, you gotta love them to work on them (pianos, I mean) because when you tune that first string, you have about 250 more to go! I used to put off adjusting the valve lash in my MG's engine because it is tedious work (eight valves), but when I get the linkage in one key working right, the piano has 87 more waiting for my attention. But I think the piano is a glorious instrument, worthy of my best efforts for however long it takes.

I used to type long letters to my mother and friends, and they said they enjoyed them. All of my English teachers said that I should write, even though they were generous with their red ink while giving me A's on themes and research papers. But I had too many other things to do. Then I got lucky, for the editor of my local paper asked me to write up a conversation we had about the former service station built by my grandfather. The resulting three paragraphs generated so much interest that he asked whether I could write more "stuff like that."

I am still writing columns for him, and as a result, the late Madelyn Green recruited me to write for this paper. My mother-in-law in Texas says that *Prime Times!* is the best newspaper she sees, because it has complete sentences, words are used right, and spelled right. The columns and magazine articles I have written have brought me many wonderful friends as well as opportunities to speak to groups (free meal usually included!) and even to teach classes.

Naturally, I recommend that you ride your hobby hard. Doing something you like to do is a good way to spend your time. It is fulfilling and rewarding, and therefore worth whatever it costs. But you might get lucky, as I did, and find that others will pay you to do something that you really like to do. And that, my friends, is a bit of Heaven on earth. Go for it!

New Food Favorites
April 2005

75 years of eating good Southern cooking has finally caught up with me. I have written columns about Southern cooking, and it now looks as if I will have to recall them. When I was learning engineering drafting in an Air Force school, our instructor gave us this bit of doggerel to practice our lettering skills:

Be careful of the words you say
    To keep them soft and sweet.
You never know from day to day
    Which ones you'll have to eat.

Little did I know then how many times I would think of those words again, *after* I had disregarded them. But columns are as perishable as the funny papers, so few there be who might remember what I have written earlier.

When I did a column I called "Everyone Else Talks Funny," I followed it with one extolling Southern cooking called "And They Cook Funny, Too." February was Heart Month, and last year I wrote a tongue-in-cheek column warning people about ordering anything on the menu with a little red valentine by it. "Chances are it will not have any butter in it, or anything else that would make it taste good and be easy to eat. No, you will struggle with barely steamed veggies, baked meat that cried out to be fried, and salads with no oil to help them slide easily down the little red lane," I wrote.

Well, my struggle has begun. I suddenly lost part of the visual field in my right eye one morning, and I spent the next hour with my eye doctor. His attentions made the clot go away in a few days, but the dark cloud remains. Then began the rounds to most of the rest of the medical profession. These visits are still in progress, so I do not have conclusions to report. But you don't want to read them anyway.

In a week, I went from a lifetime of taking almost no medicine to taking *many* little pills and capsules. I felt the only way to be sure I took them all was to buy one of those little plastic boxes with compartments labeled "a.m." and "p.m." for each day of the week. I fill up the compartments every Saturday evening after I empty that last one. The fact that such a thing was readily available seems to indicate that many folks share my plight and might still be reading this.

What will happen now? The doctors are suggesting lifestyle changes, mostly in eating habits. You know the drill, eat less and exercise more. Stop eating nearly everything I like and start eating things I will have to learn to like. Stop being a computer potato (don't watch much TV so I am not a couch potato, but I do spend a lot of time with my computer) and get out and walk more furiously. I still run up stairs because I am too impatient to climb them at a normal pace.

And that is another thing . . . need to slow down and take life easier. Isn't that the reward of retirement? Just do the things you want to do, not so many that you have to do? I have volunteered so much (the Air Force guys also tried to teach me not to do that) of my time that it is not my own any more.

Also, quit worrying and ranting about the state of the world. Can't do much about it anyway, and no one wants to hear about it from me. I don't think they want to hear about it from the TV either, but if you turn the thing on it will tell you everyone's version of it, and show you things you'd rather not see.

I hope that I will be given some time to make necessary adjustments and thus continue to enjoy life on our troubled little blue ball. One of my pastors was always quoting Robert Browning's "Grow old along with me! The best is yet to be." I sure hope he was right.

Home & Garden
May 2005

For many of us who grew up with both a home and a garden, they are practically inseparable. To be a good and complete home, it must have a good garden spot around the yard somewhere. When I have strayed from this precept, I have always been fretful about it. Why? Grass and shrubs make a house beautiful in its setting, and are certainly the norm for a city house, but the inhabitants of a house without a vegetable garden are missing out on something.

Missing from the produce counters of the great supermarkets is the wonderful flavor of vegetables allowed to develop on the growing plant, harvested and consumed at this peak of flavor. Today's produce is bred for mass production and to be harvested all at once by machinery. Tomatoes grown this way have a tough skin so the machine won't tear it, and they are picked green so they won't bruise. Once inside the packing plant, the tomatoes are run through a gas atmosphere that changes their color from green to red. Given no other choice, the produce shopper selects pretty tomatoes, all about the same size, with no blossom-end rot, no blemishes from prying insects (they won't eat that stuff, for it was not allowed to ripen!), and no distinctive tomato flavor either.

Corn is another huge beneficiary of ripening on the plant. The pot of water should be brought to a boil BEFORE the corn is pulled from the stalk. You can pick up the trail of shucks later; the point is to dine on corn that tastes sweet like corn is supposed to. The sugars in the kernels start turning to starch as soon as the ear is snapped off the stalk. There is nothing like tender, sweet corn right off the stalk.

It is the same story all the way around the produce bins. Everything is beautiful, in bright green, red, orange, yellow, purple or whatever. Nothing wilted, but kept lusciously moist and succulent so you will buy it. All of that stuff is produced by our huge agribusiness complex, aided and abetted by the agricultural departments of the world who must feed ever more and more people who do not wish to expend any sweat of their brow to eat.

We also like to shelter our house among tall trees, whose leaves help to keep it cool in summer. Unfortunately, my big maples, oaks and poplar trees do such a good job that there is not a spot anywhere on my land that gets a full day of sun. Veggies gotta have full sun to do their thing. So I am dependent on a few hardy souls who will till up a plot in spring, select the good ol' fashioned varieties that we old timers cherish, and plant a big vegetable garden. Then they rent a space at the Courthouse (Lord, we should GIVE it to them for the service they perform for humanity!), load up the tired old pick-up truck, and bring those tasty vegetables to us to pick over and try to drive a bargain. For me, I gladly pay their asking price and handle my precious vegetables like the treasures they really are.

I realize that I am fortunate indeed to have grown up on a small farm with loving grandparents who taught me how to make a good garden. Lord knows, I did not appreciate THEN having to hoe the garden and dress it, always working in the hot sun. (You grow vegetables where THEY like, not where YOU like, remember?) It is my hope that this column will remind you how good vegetables can be and that you will be able to exercise some control over what you eat. I hope that young people especially will heed this, and look to patronize the farmers who are still offering good food on our roadsides and city squares. Tell them I sent you, and don't haggle . . . smile into those careworn faces under those big straw hats that have staved off skin cancer for decades, and thank them for growing the good stuff and sharing with you.

Summer Fun
June 2005

Summer fun for most people involves water, right? Spring and Fall are generally great for enjoying outdoor activities, but when Summer really sets in, many of us decide it is too hot, humid, bright, or whatever to go outside much. We seniors get the necessary yard or gardening chores done in early morning, and then retreat to our air conditioned castles for the rest of the day, if possible.

Water is the answer to making summer tolerable, or even fun. Many head for the beach and the cooling breezes of the ocean front. Others put a boat into the sparkling water of a lake and find all kinds of ways to get wet and/or generate their own breeze to stay cool. I would like to suggest an alternative for those of us who cannot avail ourselves of either of the above: visit a waterfall!

The area covered by distribution of this magazine has waterfalls in abundance, probably more than 200 of them. As a boy growing up in Polk County, I was no more impressed by waterfalls than the coming of Spring and Fall. I mean, what's all the fuss about the azaleas or the varied colors of autumn? It does that every year, doesn't it? And anybody knows that water runs downhill . . .

Then we drove from the Dallas area to Seattle by way of the Grand Tetons and Yellowstone. I loved Jenny Lake and the falls of the Yellowstone River. After seeing the amount of water falling some 300 feet in the lower falls, I realized how much water had to be going over the upper falls that we had seen first. I was hooked and began to look for waterfalls wherever we went.

I had to see Niagara Falls. Nothing you have ever seen prepares you for the size and power of Niagara. That much water falling that far shakes the earth mightily, and the continuous roar underlies everything in the immediate area. The thing makes its own rainbow, and is always beautiful to behold, day or night.

Having seen such big waterfalls, why do I now care about the little ones we have here? Why do I take our visitors to see our nearby falls? I like them, and my friends do, too. I cannot explain the magic of falling water, but it seems to work on nearly everyone. The teen-aged daughter of friends said she'd like to come back with someone special. Ah, romance kindled and nourished by falling water!

I have a splendid view of nearby Tryon Peak and White Oak mountains from my house in Columbus. Shunkawaukan Falls tumbles off the plateau at the top of the mountain and falls in fits and starts all the way down some 2000 feet of mountain, then scurries around Columbus as Horse Creek. I can see two of the main falls, but the lower one is on private property so I have not been close to it. I take any visitor willing to drive up the mountain to the upper falls, where the creek goes under the road in a culvert, only to start falling again immediately, down the nearly sheer mountain side.

Pearson's Falls is the more celebrated of the falls near my home. It was discovered by engineer Charles Pearson while he was looking for a place to run the railroad track up the mountain. The famous Saluda Grade is another story, so fraught with danger that it has been abandoned. The Tryon Garden Club bought the Falls property from the Pearson family and maintains the glen from the nominal admission fees.

The falls and glen were severely damaged by the storm of 1993. Many of the trees were knocked down, huge boulders were redistributed, and the creek was re-routed. A massive cleanup effort resulted in reopening the glen to visitors, but it is not like it was before. Most of the trail is now sunny; it was all shady before. The plants grow bigger now, but many that thrived in the moist shade are no longer there at all. Now there are glimpses of the falls from the trail before they come into full view, but I thought it was more dramatic when they suddenly appeared in all their glory with only their sound having suggested them before.

I recommend a book called "North Carolina Waterfalls," by Kevin Adams. I bought my copy in a National Forest Service store on the Blue Ridge Parkway. Adams gives detailed directions to about 160 falls, together with photographs and how he took them. Or you may just call me, and I will direct you to Shunkawaukan and Pearson's Falls. I hope you will enjoy them as much as I do.

Antique Collectibles
July 2005

Someone gave us a souvenir pillow proclaiming "Genuine Antique Person: Been There, Done That, Don't Remember." I suppose we are antiques, since we are both on Social Security and Medicare. This will be fun to write because I know nothing about either antiques or collectibles. I do know that stuff collects in our house and gets old.

Are we antiques simply because we are older? Not necessarily. Some older things are merely old and have no remarkable features that would make them more valuable than similar older things. Antiques that do not make the cut are offered as "junque" by dealers with a sense of humor. Since one man's junk is another's antique, the dealers display all of it and hope for the best.

Our daughter started buying antiques as a child. Now an Interior Designer, she is still doing it because she recognizes the quality of the materials and craftsmanship of old. The vinyl-covered chipboard pieces of today look the best they ever will on the day they are assembled, but a dining table made of cherry is more beautiful a century later than it was when new!

Collectibles are another category altogether. We collect things. That's because we have a big house. I built a big house so there would be room to walk around the bed to make it up, and room for a dirty clothes basket next to the john. Actually, we do not mean to collect things; they just collect on all level surfaces and in all corners. That's because the closets and built-in storage cabinets are already full.

Daughter suggested leaving lots of space in our built-in bookshelves for "art objects." These include things like the carved wildebeests brought back to us from Africa by missionary friends, the ceramic whirling dervish from the Middle East, etc., to which I have added a piano player made from horse shoe nails and a "hot wheels" version of Dale Earnhardt's

No. 3 car. (Oops! Faux pas!) Anyway, the books we keep on buying in spite of having a house full of them are beginning to crowd the "art," and some books must now recline atop the others standing on the shelves from the beginning.

We have a special weakness for what I call "coffee table books." Some of these massive tomes will completely cover the average coffee table, so we bought a very large table with a glass top. However, there is the obligatory large plant in the center of the table, so any books are relegated to the edges. Since the average coffee table book is twice as big as the remaining space, they are relegated to being stacked in a large stereo cabinet nearby. Who will remove sixteen tons of books to look at the one at the bottom of the stack? Too bad.

There is also a bookcase devoted to autographed books only. Many of these were written by friends. Most people who buy my book want me to sign it, and I am more than pleased to do so. However, I advise them with a grin that writing in it will decrease its value. I learned this on a TV show about antiques and collectibles, so you see, I do know a little bit. I also learned that the price of an antique toy is greatly enhanced by the presence of the original box! I created a dust jacket for my book to help it sell itself in the stores. Like the toy box, a dust jacket in good condition adds to the value of an old book. Know, too, that there were no dust jackets when the REALLY valuable books were created!

We also have a lot of framed original art on our walls. You don't know the artists, but we do. We are supposed to be in the process of moving from our big house to a much smaller house, which means that there will not be room for most of the stuff that has collected on our walls and shelves. What to do with it? The kids don't want it, and the neighbors probably don't want it either! My plan is to move the stuff we really must keep to the smaller house, then have an "moving sale" in the big house. I suppose it will hurt a bit to see paintings go for less than the cost of the frame, and books not go at all, but all of it will have to go somewhere. We hope to realize enough from the sale to pay the man to haul away what remains. Like the antique dealer, we will display it all and hope for the best.

Sharing Vacation Memories
September. 2005

During my working years I used most of my vacation time to maintain the house and car or to visit family if we traveled. Now that we are continually on vacation (read retired) I still spend it the same way, because we still have a house and car and I have said yes to too many civic responsibilities! I am not much of a tourist, but we have managed to see most of the USA in our travels.

So how do I have Vacation Memories to share? Fran and I have just returned from a real vacation trip in celebration of our 50th wedding anniversary. Jim and Judy, whose friendship we have enjoyed for most of those years, went on a cruise to Alaska last year, and because there were problems with both weather and ship, they wanted to try it again this year. They invited us to join them, and we agreed that it was about time we did something like that.

Not being a tourist, I told them to make all the plans and that I would just tag along to look and to eat. However, Fran discovered an excursion from Juneau via small floatplanes to a remote lodge on a river for a salmon bake. As an airplane pilot, I don't like or trust helicopters, so she knew I would enjoy this trip. However, Judy does not trust airplanes smaller than a 737, but for me she gave in and booked the four of us for the salmon bake excursion.

We spent a week in the Seattle area with our friends Hal and Celia before boarding the Coral Princess at Vancouver, Canada, for a sail up the Inland Waterway. Our ports of call were Ketchikan, Juneau, Skagway, and finally Whittier, from whence a bus took us to the airport at Anchorage for our return home. The ship spent the better part of two days in Glacier Bay and College Fjord for us to see glaciers, whales and other wildlife up close.

I did buy a great new digital camera to record the looking, and among the four of us we took about 4000 photos. Our policy is to take at least two pictures every time in case someone blinks or jiggles the camera. Our album has 200 pictures, and Judy made one with more than a hundred. I had expected to cull the number to about two dozen . . . HA! We did a separate album for Mt. Rainier and Snoqualmie Falls. Hal was kind enough to drive us to all the scenic spots and to pull off the road every two minutes for the cameras to click.

Since I had unexpected quadruple by-pass heart surgery on April 1st there was some question about our going on the cruise on May 7th. I told my surgeon that since he did not want me to do anything but walk anyway, I thought I could do that on the ship and the soil of Alaska as well as that of North Carolina. My progress was so good that he told me to go ahead, so off we went without asking any more questions.

There were two large rooms full of people waiting to clear US Customs in Vancouver to board three cruise ships. One of the attendants said the wait would be several hours, so Judy told her that because of my recent surgery I could not stand that long. Magic words! The young woman immediately took the four of us to a Customs desk and we were on the ship in a matter of minutes. The ship sailed while we were having dinner a few hours later.

When our little plane landed on the Taku River near Taku Lodge after flying very close to the snow covered peaks and the glaciers, Judy gave me a bear hug and thanked me for requesting the floatplane trip. She loved it! The salmon was great, too, but it was probably the most expensive lunch we ever ate. A bear came and cleaned up the grill (no food left outside the lodge) and that added to our enjoyment.

Jim provided another highlight of our trip when he drove a rental car into the Yukon so we could stop at every pullout to take pictures of the grandeur of the rivers, lakes and mountain peaks. My camera has a superb zoom lens that allows me to pull things close, but I found that I used the extreme wide angle setting most often to capture as much of the scene as possible. The road and the railroad track are the only works of man visible in that vast wilderness of unspoiled natural beauty that seemed to stretch for hundreds of miles in all directions.

We got rained on in Ketchikan, and Anchorage was overcast all day, but we had remarkably good weather all other days. We would start out with sweaters and jackets against the wind and cold, but the layers came off rather quickly as the sun warmed things up. The sun rose early and set late up there at some 60 degrees latitude. We enjoyed very long days with plenty of sunshine for picture taking, but always enough clouds in the sky to make them interesting.

We enjoyed having four English widows as our dinner companions for the entire cruise. They travel almost continually, especially to France and Italy since they are so close to England. We shared many stories of people and places, but also many dining experiences. As we give directions around the Carolinas in terms of restaurants, so did they about Europe. One of them told us about seeing a bear scratching his back on a tree, providing body undulations and expressions of ecstasy that were delightfully uninhibited.

I told the ladies about my late friend Pete, a former RAF pilot who came to California to marry the girl he met while in flight training there during WWII. Pete was a great storyteller, and when he had had a few beers at parties we could get him to recite Robert Service's epic poem, "The Cremation of Sam McGee." I picked up a copy of it in Carcross, Yukon, and the ladies accepted my invitation to read it to them after breakfast.

A by-product of my surgery has been a lack of appetite and poor digestion. I am the only person they know in cardiac rehab that weighed the same before and after a cruise! I like being at my target weight already, and not carrying that extra 35 pounds of lard any more. But I would have liked to enjoy all that wonderful food they kept bringing to our table on the ship. We liked our waiter, too . . . the more so when we learned his "code." If he did not say

"Excellent choice!" when you ordered, it was good to ask for his recommendation. His approval meant an excellent second choice indeed.

All of the Alaskans we met were friendly and courteous, remarkable when you consider that the cruise ships increased the population of their port towns ten fold when present. There were probably as many seasonal workers as full time residents, all dedicated to making our visit memorable. Indeed it was, and we brought back about two thousand memory aids. Now we have to write captions for them while we still remember names and locations!

The Apples of My Eye
September 2005

I suppose I am pretty fickle, because I can think of a whole tree full of Apples of my Eye! First and foremost is my wife, followed by the kids and grandkids, and then there are all those toys I have loved over the years.

Like Charlie Brown, I have always fancied girls with red hair. They are a special breed; they tend to set themselves apart from other girls in ways that I find appealing. I like their fierce independence and total confidence. I was lucky enough to win my chosen "little red haired girl," and have no regrets after more than fifty years together. Fran has not yet given up on trying to make me acceptable in society.

We adopted our children when they did not come naturally. They don't have my genes, but they sure have some good ones! For those reasons, I feel free to brag on them at any opportunity. Our boy Thomas and I locked horns early on as the young bull began his quest to replace the old bull, but now we are friends. We still get into heated discussions about some world issues, but we agree on more stuff than not these days. He keeps another of my apples polished, but more about that later.

Our girl Sharon is another matter. She reached up from her crib, grabbed my little finger, and has held on ever since. We never really locked horns; she would just tell me politely that she could not listen to any more about that right then. She is still polite when she tells me how it is going to be. Now she has given us the sweetest and smartest little girl we know, and a very determined little boy who could smack a ball clear across the yard with a bat before he was three. More apples!

Fran's brother offered me his MGB when he reentered college after his Navy service, and since I had enjoyed driving the sports cars that some of my friends had, I accepted. What fun we all had in that little blue car! It was a GT with a little seat behind ours that was perfect for the kids. With only one seatbelt in back, they slid back and forth under it as I took all turns at maximum speed. I am happy that both of them got to drive its successors and learn how much fun driving a responsive car can be.

I learned to fly airplanes with Oscar Meyer at the Hendersonville airport right after WWII, and owned a succession of them, too. My favorite was a red and white Luscombe that I flew enough hours to feel at home in. I made a box for the kids to sit on in the Buick and the airplane so they would be tall enough to look out the window. I took them up often when they were small, one at a time because the Luscombe had only two seats, side-by-side.

On a trip from Texas over to Louisiana to see Uncle Ethan, a gust rocked the plane over Tyler, and when I moved the control stick to correct, Thomas saw his stick move. He reached forward, grabbed it with both hands, and began to stir it around. He was delighted with the results as the little plane wobbled about, but I had to tell him not to do that, so he promptly went to sleep. He switched to motorcycles when he grew up.

One Sunday afternoon, Sharon spent the first five minutes of her turn trying to unwrap a cheese cracker and then stuff the wrapping somewhere, so I just landed and went on home (she was only about a year old). Later I tried again in a rented aerobatic airplane, and had to turn around to see how she was doing in the back seat. She had both arms outstretched and was fluttering her lips to make engine sounds. She was always ready to go flying with Dad after that.

However, the MG experience prevailed, and she insisted on stick shifts in the first few cars she bought.

I traded an engineer friend a ride in my Luscombe, including loops and spins, for a ride in his sailboat. Soon I was the proud owner of a Sunfish, a 14-foot day sailer with planing hull. Thomas sailed that more than I did, but Sharon did not care to take a zig-zag course to sail into the wind. For me, sailing is almost as much fun as flying. After all, the sail functions much as the wing of an airplane does!

After being retired for a while, I decided I did not need two cars. I was working on the MG more than driving it, and the Buick was going to need expensive repairs, so I sold both and got a new Saturn. This nimble little car handles much like the MG and has most of the comforts of the Buick, like leather bucket seats and air conditioning. I opted for a silver or gold sedan, but my now white-haired Fran showed her true colors and insisted on a red station wagon. Excellent choice! Now if we could just get it to rise a bit to meet us when we get into it . . .

When Thomas started his auto detailing business, he did our Saturn for us. He told me that to call my car a "pig sty" would be "an insult to the pig!" I used to spend every Saturday morning prettying up my car, but now I just put in gas and oil and drive it. It is our family car, our pick-up truck and my sports car. It goes wherever we need to go and takes whatever we need to take, rain or shine. That's what makes it another apple on a very full tree. I hope you are also blessed with a bountiful apple crop.

A Life-Changing Moment
October 2005

On January 28 in early morning, I combed my hair as usual, then started to get dressed. A dark area suddenly appeared in the upper part of my visual field! It did not go away as I put on my clothes, and I discovered that the shadow was in my right eye only. My eye doctor discovered a blood clot and worked for an hour trying to move it off my optic nerve.

In April, I wrote about having to recall my columns extolling the virtues of Southern cooking because that blood clot led to visits to other doctors in a matter of days and tests to see what other problems I might have. "What will happen now?" I wrote. "The doctors are suggesting lifestyle changes, mostly in eating habits . . ."

What happened was some seven hours of surgery in which one of my carotid arteries was cleaned out, four blocked arteries to my heart were by-passed with a vein taken from my leg, and many holes were drilled by laser beams in the damaged area of my heart to allow blood to seep in once more. I am happy to report that I knew nothing of any of this and felt no pain before, during or after.

When the folks at Asheville Cardiology finished their testing, they could not believe that I had had no pain and no symptoms. With long faces they told me about the problems and the necessary surgery. After surgery, the doctors and nurses at the Mission Memorial Heart center told me with big smiles what a wonderful recovery I was making, when in fact I had no appetite and whatever I ate seemed to form a knot in my stomach.

This poor digestion continued for some two months, but the good news is that I got down to my target weight right away and have maintained it now that I am eating again. Trouble is, the things the doctors want me to eat taste funny, or just plain bad! Wife Fran dutifully baked a loaf of "whole grain" bread for me, but it had a "whang" to it that penetrated whatever good-tasting food was eaten with it. She also made up some Good Seasons Italian dressing with olive oil and that was pretty wild, too. Does anyone LIKE olive oil?

We bought some "fat free" Ranch dressing by the Hidden Valley people, who invented Ranch dressing. There was no warning label stating that the stuff would not taste anything like their Ranch dressing. I like iceberg lettuce and thoroughly dislike Romaine and Endive, because of their strong flavors. The diet lady says that iceberg lettuce has little food value, but I eat it for fiber, not vitamins!

I have learned to eat oatmeal, but it still gets bigger and bigger the longer I try to chew it. Friend Judy says she has never before seen anyone chew oatmeal, but I learned in the eighth grade that digestion begins in the mouth while food is chewed to mix saliva with it, so I give everything my best shot. Never in my life had indigestion until my recent surgery! So bear with me while I roll the stuff around a while before sending it down the hatch.

Why is everything that is low in fat also high in sodium? When I do find something that has neither, it also has no taste. Since I am taking lots of expensive meds to control my blood chemistry and pressure, I should not eat things that work against my meds, right? But what about meds that require other meds to counter their effects? Not for me, but I had to "go 'round and 'round" with my doctors to stop that foolishness.

I am just finishing 36 sessions of Cardiac Rehab at Pardee. There I met a roomful of new people, some working with us to rebuild our muscles and endurance, and the rest working out and learning as I am. All of us are trying to make the most of our new lease on life, and our mentors are pleased with our progress. Did I fit in with this group? Well, I sold them several Lions brooms and copies of my book!

New friend Ray learned to fly airplanes with Oscar Meyer at the Hendersonville airport as I did, so we are always exchanging pilot talk about the workout machines. I named the Nu-Step machine "F-15 Fighter Jet" because its big pedals remind me of the F-15's rudder pedals. I would invite Ray, over on a nearby Nu-Step ("The F-16"), to try to catch me and join up in formation. I would also accuse our squadron commander Joel of disabling the aileron boost on my plane because I was having to work too hard. Is rehab fun, or what?

I gave one of my books to my heart surgeon, and this is what I wrote in it: "I was a stranger and ye took me in (Matthew 25:35 KJV). There were no questions about my background, achievements, or character. I needed the help you could give, and you made arrangements to extend my life at a renewed level. All you have asked is that I take better care of myself, and I shall certainly try to do that." I owe Dr. Ely that much, don't you think?

Wartime Memories
November 2005

For most senior citizens more than 70 years old, wartime means WWII. Though there have been many conflicts involving the United States since then, they were not officially called "wars" going in, but some were after they escalated in size and scope. As with the recent attack on the World Trade Center buildings, everyone remembers exactly where they were and what they were doing when they heard about the Japanese attack on Pearl Harbor that put the United States officially and totally into WWII.

There are always persons who oppose going to war for any reason, or perhaps just for the reason at hand, but I believe that there would not be a United States of America as we know it had we not prevailed in the Revolutionary War, the Civil War, WWII, and the Cold War. I am not as sure about the other conflicts, but I feel that we must always be on guard against any who threaten our country from within or without.

I was eleven years old, visiting my fourth grade teacher with my mother, when the news of Pearl Harbor came on the radio. My late father had served in the Army in Hawaii before they met, so Mother got out his scrapbooks to show my younger brother and me. Uncles, aunts and cousins went off to war, and we went to school where we followed the events unfolding in both Europe and the Pacific. Older boys enlisted and some people left the area to work in defense plants.

Unlike more recent conflicts, the whole country was committed to winning WWII. Nearly every family had someone directly involved in the war effort. We got ration books with little stamps for food and gasoline. We collected scrap metal in a big pile at school; even household grease was recycled into war materiel. Production of automobiles and household appliances was halted for "the duration," a new term meaning until the war was over. The War dominated our lives and our thinking, because we were all affected.

We were told about the fighting by "war correspondents," whose words came to us from overseas via short wave radio that rose and fell, came and went, in waves of sound and background noise. Newspapers and magazines carried printed words and pictures some time after the fact, but there were "newsreels" at the local movie theatre that were fairly timely. All the news was slanted pro-Allies and anti-Axis, with our few early victories hailed as indicators that we would surely prevail ultimately over the forces of our enemies. Military secrecy and censorship were honored because everyone understood that "loose lips sink ships."

As a young teen, I wanted to fly a B-17 "Flying Fortress" and do my part to knock out Hitler's war machine. The big bomber was so named for its many machine guns, but it proved unable to defend itself adequately and many planes and crews were lost before long-range fighter escorts became available. When I later learned to fly airplanes, I realized I would rather have flown a P-51 fighter plane. One of my cousins did fly the B-17 and later commanded a B-29 in combat over Japan. In response to her question, he told my mother that it was sort of like sitting on the porch and flying the house.

Britain's Winston Churchill always flashed the two-finger "V for Victory" sign whenever he appeared in public to inspire determination to win the war at any cost. The opening bars of Beethoven's 5th symphony tap out the Morse code for "V" (...—), so it was played often by our side, even though Beethoven was German. Since he scratched out the dedication of his 3rd Symphony to Napoleon when he made himself emperor, I think Beethoven would have approved the Allied victory over his errant homeland.

The terms of the WWI armistice provided that Germany could not build airplanes or other machines of war. So they built gliders to train their pilots—at first. But they eventually designed airplanes and tanks that were superior to ours and built them in quantity because there was no one to stop them. One reason we eventually won the war was that our bombers blew up the sources of fuel for the Nazi war machine. We also finally had more of everything than they had.

WWII changed the whole world, mostly for the better. New countries were born as the former European kingdoms gave up their colonies. We rebuilt the countries and the economies of our former enemies. But even today there are families in our country that are smaller because some of their brothers did not come home with them. As you enjoy your freedom to criticize our Government and do pretty much as you please, think of what that cost so many families right around you. And please don't increase the price by giving aid and encouragement to those who even now want us dead and are willing to kill themselves to achieve it!

Those people see our America as the "Great Satan," and American television (seen all over the world!) seems to try to prove them right with what now passes for music and entertainment. Those getting rich from this activity scream about censorship and First Amendment rights if anyone dares to point out what I just did.

Most of us understood the consequences of losing WWII, and we were determined that we would not. Does anyone understand what we may be losing now by refusing to heed the lessons offered by God and by history?

An Incredible Gift
December 2005

Why is Christmas a season of giving? I think it is because the "greatest gift ever" (editor's topic) was given to us about this time some two thousand years ago. Our Creator, who gave us "unalienable rights" according to Jefferson's Declaration, also gave us choices. Why did He do that?

Well, I think it is because He had everything else. He had made hosts of angels to worship him without question and to do his bidding. Everything He had made worked perfectly and did just what He expected. He decided to make a creature much like himself, of limited ability and knowledge, but free to do whatever he pleased. If His new creature chose to worship Him, that would be great. He called His new friend Adam and placed him in a beautiful Garden. He made other creatures and plants and let Adam name them.

Adam and his God walked together in the Garden in the cool of the evening and enjoyed each other's company. For a while. Then Adam asked for someone more like himself to keep him company the rest of the time, and God gave him a woman friend called Eve. He also gave them some rules to follow so they might live happily ever after in fellowship with Him.

These two were smart enough to want to know more, so they chose to break the rules and do their own thing. Bad idea! For there were Consequences. The worst of these was that God could no longer have fellowship with them. This would not do, for God loved them and still wanted to enjoy their friendship.

How to fix it? It took a while (in our perception of time) and much experimentation with new rules, selective destruction, "chosen" people, punishment and rewards, until it grieved God that he had ever made mankind, since man's "only thoughts were only evil continually" (His words).

But finally God sent His son Jesus into the world to live among us and show us the way. Some saw Jesus as a threat to their own power and authority and contrived to kill Him. They thought they had succeeded, but in fact Jesus as the Christ gave His own life for us, and then returned to His Father. He had told those who would listen that He was going to prepare a place for them with His Father. He has also told all of us how to join them there when our life here ends.

We may choose to follow Jesus or to go our own way, both now and hereafter. God's gift of eternal life with Him is free to all, for we cannot buy it or earn it. To receive this incredible gift, however, we must choose Jesus now, for there is no opportunity hereafter! Those who follow Christ Jesus are called Christians, and we celebrate His birth at Christmas.

If you are a Christian, send Christmas cards, not Season's Greetings! Tell the world the Reason for the Season! Jesus gave us few "rules," but one of them is to tell others about Him. If we truly love Him and believe in Him, can we do any less?

* * * * * *

The owner of *Prime Times!* locked the doors at the end of December 2005 and the staff found themselves unemployed.

The Communication of Love
Just a column idea, not published . . .

The communications of love are as varied as the people communicating. Or attempting to.

In the USA, both male and female students take the same English courses in the same classrooms, but when they try to communicate they use a foreign language or a code to which the other has no key. If I could view the multitude of my readers now, I believe I would see both of them nodding in agreement with the same look of bewilderment and resignation. Therefore I will not offer examples.

When words are spoken face to face, there is some opportunity to break the code by observing facial expression or noting the tone of voice. But writing is very dangerous because both of these clues are unavailable. People read between the lines or put ideas into the words that might have never occurred to the writer. We put little smiley faces in our e-mails now, hoping thereby to convey the idea that we are not serious about what we just wrote.

Technology has given us many ways to express love in words, but neither the telephone, the FAX machine, the Internet chat room, nor personal ads address the language problem I mentioned. The words go more quickly or more plainly, but the interpretation of them is a problem, compounded further by outright fraud or intended deception. A deliberately provocative ad in the personals by a "black female" brought in hundreds of responses from men, who discovered that the Humane Society was trying to place a Labrador retriever in a good home.

The language of love goes far beyond words. If it were not so, many of us males would never know love. We cannot all woo like Cyrano de Bergerac or look like Robert Redford, so we must rely on other means to attract and keep a mate. Consideration and respect go a long way. Taking out the trash and mopping the kitchen floor will lead to a warmer reception at bedtime than anything we might say.

When I moved away over the Christmas holidays, I sent my former fourth grade classmates a letter telling them about my new home and school. All of them replied in letters telling me about their Christmas and all of them signed "Love." All the boys and all the girls! My complimentary close was "Your friend." I still remember many of them after all these years, for I suppose I loved them, too.

February is the Month for Lovers
By Fran Goodwin

February has long been the month for lovers. Perhaps someone of great wisdom decided that February was a very dreary month in the dead of winter and something needed to be done to cheer it up.

Valentine's Day was probably derived from the ancient Roman holiday feast Lupercalia. This was the day young Roman men and women drew names for a partner for the coming year in lottery form. Gradually it became associated with the feast day February14, named for two Roman martyrs both named Valentine. Cards and gifts are exchanged now to show affection and love. The greeting card makers clean up this time of year, as do the chocolate makers.

The holiday is also associated with the legend of birds that mate for life. Cards are often decorated with doves and swans, two birds that mate for life. Would not it be nice if people mated for life?

My first gift from my future husband was a paperweight of marble holding a brass copy of the clasped hands of Robert and Elizabeth Barrett Browning. (The original hands are at the Browning Museum on the campus of Baylor University in Waco, Texas.) This was a very special gift to me and still is after 48 years. The paperweight graces my desk, right beside my computer where I see it each time I sit there.

In the Middle Ages, young ladies did very fine handwork to show their love for some young Lochinvar, especially when he went oft to fight dragons or whatever to show his love for the young lady. A knight wore near to his heart or on his sleeve, a scarf with the name of his loved one and perhaps a heart and flowers that she had embroidered, hence the saying, "He wears his heart on his sleeve." This would show everyone just how much he cared for his lady.

Maybe we need to slow down and think more of our Lochinvars or perhaps Janes and make something special just for them. (Handwork is not something that just ladies do.) During the time I am stitching for a certain person 1 think about them and what they mean to me. I think of bad times as well as good times. The bad times make the good times even better.

The above article was published in Prime Times! *issue of February 2002.*

Mason & Hamlin Story
By Garland O. Goodwin *(previously unpublished)*

The Air Force sent me to Barksdale Field near Shreveport, Louisiana, after they closed the school in which I had become an instructor. With my great enthusiasm for airplanes, I naturally spent a lot of my off-duty time wandering around the flight line and nosing into the big hangars. In one of them I found, not airplanes, but a bowling alley. Enough light came in through the big open doors for me to spot a large grand piano in a corner of a stage. I had had enough piano lessons to be playing several classical pieces from memory, so I pounced on that piano immediately.

There was no one around to hear or care, so I played everything I knew and more besides, just to hear the wonderful sound the piano produced. I did not know the name on the fallboard (even then, at 19 years of age, I had developed a decided preference for Steinway pianos), but I was favorably impressed by the full but even tone of this large piano. It was a Mason & Hamlin concert grand, a full nine feet long, with really big fat hammers, especially in the bass.

I had written out a solo piano arrangement of the first movement, first theme, of the Tchaikovsky Piano Concerto in B-flat minor, but had not had an opportunity to learn to play it. I spent a lot of time playing it on that piano, plus re-learning my other pieces and some new ones after I sent home for my music books. Hardly anyone ever stopped in to ask me to play something, and no one ever told me not to play the piano, so I enjoyed having essentially my very own concert grand until I was transferred!

A year or so after I left, I managed to get a hop to Barksdale, and went looking for that piano. Its former hangar home now had airplanes in it, so I went over to the Service Club to while away the time until my plane was to leave. There I found it on the stage, looking great. I asked about it, and the WAF on duty told me that a Captain somebody had to approve anyone playing it, and that he was flying that day. So I did not get to play it again, but I was glad to see that it was then being cared for properly.

That experience was the beginning of my appreciation for differences in piano tone qualities that are "built into" the instruments. Since those days I have played many other fine instruments by many different makers, all equally dedicated to producing musical instruments with inspiring tone and responsive actions. I am especially pleased that a goodly number of the truly great pianos of a century ago are being made again by people dedicated to quality so that their distinctive voices may be heard today.

A Steinway among Steinways
By Garland O. Goodwin *(previously unpublished)*

While a student on the GI Bill I decided that I wanted a piano. On a bright Saturday morning I entered the premises of the Los Angeles Steinway dealer to look for one. Though out of practice, I still leaned over a few keyboards and attempted a few bits of music.

Soon a snooty salesman appeared, and responded to my query about a used piano by directing me to their warehouse a few blocks away. There I found the door open, so I wandered in. I found a few workmen and dozens of pianos in various stages of assembly.

There were rows and rows of both verticals and grands almost filling the huge building.

No one took much notice of my arrival beyond a few murmured greetings of some sort. I told the nearest workman that I wanted to try out some pianos, and he said help yourself, indicating the whole place with a grand sweep of his hand. So I began my quest.

I found several uprights that would do fine, and played maybe a whole piece on some of them. There were no prices and no salesmen (warehouse, remember?) so I soon began to try the grands that were set up on their legs instead of lying on their side at rest. Soon Mr. Keith Hardesty appeared and asked me what I thought of the grand I was trying to play.

I quickly summarized for him the instrument's strengths and weaknesses, and he listened with interest. You should realize that Mr. Hardesty was a master piano technician and piano builder who had probably heard every major concert artist and many of the piano students from the music schools in the LA area. Yet he was interested in the comments of this obviously rank amateur about his pianos as we went from one to another. I have always had opinions about pianos.

One Steinway that was very good indeed, but which I thought had a rather thin treble section and weak bass, had belonged to Jascha Heifetz. Mr. Heifetz was a fine pianist himself, but was better known for his mastery of the violin. When even this piano failed to get a 100% mark from this brash youth, Mr. Hardesty decided to show me one that was in a back corner by itself and covered.

He pulled off the cover, opened the top, and got me a bench. It was an ebonized Steinway model B, usually referred to as a "seven-foot" grand, but named "Music Room Grand" by Steinway. It looked new, but was very easy to play. In fact, the more I played the better it got. I tried everything, and that piano was more than one dared to hope for. Grace notes could be dropped in without effort. I could start a crescendo and never run out of piano before I had carried the phrase over the top. It would whisper or it would roar, and anything between. Whatever I did, it did. Embarrassing—I could not blame anything on the piano. The tone was inspiring and even across the entire scale, the action was very responsive and even. The treble just sparkled with life, the bass was full and rich, yet open. And the tenor area that is muddy and dull and uninspiring on so many pianos just carried me away with its open tone and singing quality.

Mr. Hardesty returned to the piano when I finally stopped playing, and I could only tell him through tears of joy that I found that piano to be "Perfect. A Steinway among Steinways. The best piano I have ever played, or heard." Turns out it had belonged to Artur Rubinstein, and it had come in the week before when Mr. Rubinstein had closed his Hollywood home. I learned on a later visit that it had been bought by MGM studios for $4500 (c.1955.) I had not had sense enough to put a deposit on it (the price was almost a year's pay for a beginning engineer), but the privilege of playing it was priceless, an experience that I shall always treasure in memory.

Name Dropper
Or, **How PTG Helped Me Become a Piano Technician**
By Garland O. Goodwin, RPT #4173
Published in two parts by the Piano Technicians Journal, *for Nov and Dec 2003*

Why and how would an aeronautical engineer become a piano technician? The answer I am going to give you is a tribute to some of PTG's [Piano Technicians Guild] finest, many of whom are just names to our younger members.

My background: I started learning to play pianos when I was 17 years old, and owned a succession of less-than-satisfactory instruments over the years. I set about putting them right myself, since the tuners I called just tuned them and left. The first time my future mother-in-law saw me, I had her piano strewed all over her living room. Fortunately, it worked better after that.

My company sent me to Seattle for a year, so I decided to rent a piano. I found George Morgan's store, where he sold used pianos and rented out hundreds of them. I was impressed by the workmen there, who leveled keys and carefully regulated actions of the old uprights that rented for about $10 or $15 a month (1966).

A few years later, I found and bought an 1898 Steinway upright. When I discovered that it had a rosewood case, I knew I had to do this job right for my daughter. I wrote George, and he sent me a three-page letter of advice, typed, single-spaced. He also included a signed application for me to join PTG as a Student member. With an application signed by the national Immediate Past President, I was shooed right in!

At my local chapter I soon met Stuart Conner, a recent graduate of the Bob Perkins school. Stuart had taken all the courses there, including player pianos and reed organs. He agreed to take me on as his apprentice, partly because his shop was full of pianos needing everything. He was a patient and forgiving teacher, as I did things like letting a brass pedal get gouged by the guard around the buffing wheel. Also important, I learned that I did not want to get involved with either player pianos or reed organs (with them, you have to fix all or nothing.)

Stuart was a great believer in PTG and took me to several regional conferences in Ohio and

Pennsylvania. In Dayton, Ohio, I met Jack Krefting (later Tech Ed of the *Journal*) and Jim Geiger. I attended a tuning class taught by George Defebaugh, who was immediately challenged to do one of his famous "quickie" temperament settings for us. The piano was a little spinet, just like the one I had recently struggled with to pass my Apprentice test, so I was all ears as George began to place his magic tuning lever on the pins. One touch and the proper beat rates just jumped out at us. In 1:42 he had a temperament in that piano that I would have been ecstatic to tune out from! The master made it look and sound EASY.

Of the several Pennsylvania conferences we attended, my favorite was the one in Lancaster. My wife had lunch from the nearby Farmers' Market waiting for me in our room when I got out of the last morning class. Yum! There I met Dick Bittinger, who furnished a little grand piano for Victor Benvenuto to put a new soundboard in. That was a new thing for most technicians at that time, and Vic had it all figured out for us.

Edwin Trefz (of the famous piano supply house in Philadelphia) demonstrated for us the preparation of the grand rim to receive the new board. Someone asked Ed how long it took him to sharpen his big chisel. He thought a bit, as he did when answering every question, and then said "about two minutes. I used to take about five minutes, but then I discovered that after three minutes of use it was about as sharp as I could get it in two." When asked how he knew when to sharpen the chisel, he said that when you are tempted to pick up a mallet to hit the chisel, it is time to sharpen it.

My first National Convention was the one in Hollywood FL in 1975. Now that was surely a piano person's heaven on earth! So many classes, so little time! I needed to take them ALL, of course, but there was no way. Being an engineer, I was also interested in why and whether as well as how.

I scheduled a private tuning tutoring session with Dan Mensing of the Chicago chapter. I still set my temperament in the order he suggested because it works for me. A to the fork (most tuners were then using a C fork, and setting an F-F temperament from the fifth with the C. Dale said we want A-440 on the money, so we start there.) then the A octave, then the third with F (nice, warm beat rate. George Defebaugh observed that the "vibrato of the piano" is in the thirds and sixths.) Check the A octave with the third-tenth. Next tune the F octave and the three major thirds within that (beats progressing nicely.) Then tune fourths and fifths to complete the temperament. If one of the notes tuned earlier does not seem right, you have a better idea what to "fix." Final check is the smooth progression of the thirds. Unfortunately, Dan died a short time later.

Since I had difficulty determining whether the fourths and fifths were wide or narrow, I went to Virgil Smith's class about using fast-beating intervals to test the slow-beating ones. Revelation! I could hear and understand. It works! I also marveled at his perfect unisons and clean octaves; surely another master of our art. Have to get a private session with him when I get more experience!

I was so impressed with Jim Coleman's (Sr.) class that I asked him if he were an engineer, too. He was the first person I heard that got all of the engineering terms like stress, strain and tension etc. right. He smiled and asked why I asked. He smiled even bigger when I told him why, and then allowed as how he had no formal engineering training. He sent me to Lew Herwig to get more answers than he could give me, and Lew sent me to McFerrin's and Benade's books on Acoustics. Lew and Bud Corey teamed on a restringing class, and I will always remember how easily Bud leveled the pins with a BIG hammer. Bud could string eight vertical backs a day in the factory.

Several of his classes later, I observed to Jim Coleman that I considered him at least an equal to me in the fine art of "bullshipping." What could he say? He did smile again, though. [The *Journal* editors, perhaps wisely, left out this paragraph in the magazine.]

Then it was off to see Cliff Geers regulate a newly rebuilt grand action. Mash those center rail felt punchings down good (with a special lever tool he had made) before you try to level the keys. Bed the keyframe. Travel and fit the hammers before regulating let-off, drop, etc. But do everything in the right order so you don't have to repeat anything. I took good notes because it was coming too fast and furious to remember it all!

Cliff was one of Baldwin's treasures, and another was Willard Sims, a "natural-born" teacher who shared his thorough understanding of wood as well as piano technology. I always attended his classes until Baldwin assigned him elsewhere. Our loss.

The next year I got my private time with Virgil Smith. He helped me greatly with tuning lever techniques and hearing beats. Of course, I was not capable of tuning at his level (how many are?), but he patiently headed me in the right direction. Where but PTG could you go one-on-one with the very best, and for about a tuning fee?

I also went to Stephen Jellen's class. I think it was about action regulation, but I quickly realized that I was in the presence of a great master of piano technology. There was usually a tip offered as an aside to nearly everything he had planned to cover. To avoid stripping or wearing out the holes for flange and other screws going into wood, start by turning the screw backward until it clicks, then turn it into the old threads without making new ones. I still do that all the time, with ALL threaded connections (by not doing that, an engineer friend stripped two spark plug holes in the aluminum head of his Mercedes! $$$!)

Another time Steve passed around a vertical piano wippen, jack etc. mounted on short rails fastened to a pot metal action bracket. He asked if anyone could make it work. No way! He then told us that with age some brackets "grow" so that the resultant greater action spread renders the function of the action impossible. How else could we have known that? He also told us not to rob a wippen or other part from note 88 to make a key work in the middle of the piano, because Aunt Maude, who does not know a note of music, will strike note 88 and loudly declare that it does not work! Rob the highest or lowest B-flat instead, and probably no one will ever know.

Steve never had enough time to share all of his wisdom born of experience. I never missed his classes after that, and soon Wally Brooks was doing most of the talking with a weary Steve continually adding insights from his chair. Steve prepared Wally to receive his mantle by having him build several pianos from scratch. The last time I saw Steve was at Dallas in 1977 and I was shocked to see but a shadow of his former self. His cancer took him about a month later, but with Wally's help, he had literally given us all that he had.

Steve selected his disciple well, for all of us now attend Wally's classes on any subject because we know we will learn something new and valuable. Wally shows and tells, as all great teachers do, and he builds our confidence that maybe we can do that, too.

Ernie Juhn warned us to check a piano out in the owner's presence before starting to work, so they could not say later that "it wasn't doing that before you came!" He also told us to look for buzzes and rattles in the light fixture and china cabinet as well as in the piano itself.

Norman Neblitt is a master teacher of tone regulation. He would show us how to transform a mediocre sounding piano into one of powerful singing tone. From him I learned that the needles come last, that there is a world of work to do before we needle hammers. I don't know how many times he patiently worked on a hammer until everyone was satisfied that he got the most it could give. He seemed to have a treatment for every hammer ill, and gave us the confidence to attempt to do the things he did. He also did a fabulous class on that little box on grands that the pedals stick out of.

Norm had a wealth of illustrative stories, but he had to tell some disruptive attendees that if they wanted to tell stories, they should get their own class! One of my favorites of his was about the lady who told him to "do something" about "that E." Norm checked it against its neighbors and found that their tones were even, so he asked what the problem was. The lady said that her husband always sat down when he got home from work and played "that damned Fur Elise" until supper was ready.

I kept running into Jim Geiger at conventions, usually having a meal with him and his family. I always intended to pay for his supper, but he always managed to pay for mine instead. Even though I did not intend ever to move pianos, I attended one of his classes on that subject. Had no idea how much there was to consider in protecting the piano, the movers, and people's floors! Jim said NOT to wear a belt buckle that could gouge a piano's finish; Jim was wearing a "jump suit" that had no belt.

And who can think of a jump suit without having Ben McKlveen come to mind. Ben was everywhere in his trademark blue jumpsuit, teaching all subjects. At Minneapolis, Ben did a tuning concert on a big Bosendorfer Imperial grand, and of course I was there to see how to handle those extra notes at the lower end of the scale. Ben used a 14th (I think; an octave plus a seventh) as a check to compare beat rates. This also works on lesser pianos!

At our 25th Anniversary convention in Washington DC, the patron saint of PTG lamented to me that a Washington newspaper had put words into his mouth that he would never say. John Travis was not happy that they had added a gratuitous "Hell" to a supposed quote. I never heard him say anything like that, and he told me more about restringing than the scales in his book.

Bill Stegeman left us the best diagrams I have ever seen for illustrating the matching partials we use in tuning. I use Bill's diagrams when I teach about partials. I also made a pair of sliding charts to place against the fallboard to locate the partials of any two notes to show the coincident ones. Bill's class was an absolute MUST, especially for a beginning tuner.

Fred and Mimi Drasche were always in the Steinway booth and I was always in one of his classes. Fred faithfully and patiently showed us how to deal with those Teflon® bushings and the unique Steinway sostenuto mechanism. That pedal is probably the least used, and most problematic, thing on a grand piano. Oh well, we have to make it work right if we want to call ourselves piano technicians!

Fred had stories to tell, too. He told us of leaving an alcohol burner burning in the bed of a big grand when he went to get something. He returned to find the stretcher on fire, got help in putting it out, and did not lose his job at Steinway. I think that incident shows how much Fred was valued by everyone who knew him. While we are thinking about Steinway, one thing I learned from Franz Mohr was a good use for the short lid prop: Franz swung it down and hung his coat on it. Now you know.

I went to Webb Phillips' class to learn how to repair finishes and to get some ideas of how to refinish my rosewood Steinway. I learned about using lace curtains to rub black filler into the grain to enhance a figured wood before finishing it, and to get it stained like you want it before adding the protective coating. Webb is an expert in industrial finishes, and some of the stuff he recommended to us was available only in 5-gallon buckets or 55-gallon drums. I suggested to him that he buy the big amounts and repackage it in smaller sizes so we could buy (from him) only what we might use, so I like to think that I helped him get started in his now-flourishing supply business.

When Dr. Al Sanderson brought out his Accu-Tuner I had to see what that was about, so I went to a class where George Defebaugh and Jim Coleman (Sr.) each did a pitch raise on a couple of old uprights that were more than a half-step down. George did his piano aurally and Jim did his with an Accu-Tuner, each in turn explaining what they were doing as they went. I shall always remember with delight their finale: They both started at the bass end of their piano and played each note together to the top. Then they shook hands and bowed to us, to applause that was loud and long.

I learned about inharmonicity from Dr. Earle Kent himself, and then went on to Dr. Dave Roberts to see what to do with it. As an engineer, scale design (and redesign!) was right up my alley. I used my programmable TI calculator to teach classes at my local chapter and neighboring ones. I suggested some scale changes at the breaks of small grands, and calculated scales for early and no-name grands that came into their shops with no strings at all, for my fellow technicians.

Chris Robinson brought a huge grand action model to his class. He then helped us to understand the function of each part by taking it out of the action to see whether it still worked. He also showed us what happens at the extremes of all adjustments. If it is getting better, why not go all the way? He brought along a frequency analyzer to prove some of his points. When Chris asked whether the hammer flange pinning affected the tone, I was the only one to answer "yes," because I figured that if the answer were "no" he would not have brought it up! He then showed us the differences in the strength and distribution of the partials when the note was played again after loosening the bushings in the flange (so that everything else would be the same.)

I sat and listened for a good while in Nick Gravagne's grand rebuilding class, then suddenly picked up my pen to write down something he said. Nick noticed, and stopped to say to the class that I had just learned something, and went on to talk about that being why we continue to go to classes. Nick understood that he was doing everything the way I did it up to that point, so I had not taken any notes.

Of course, I am still going to Chapter meetings and our regional conference, where I learn as well as teach. I am still "getting" as I try to "give back." The icing on the cake is that Don Valley, Jim Harvey, Sammy Smith and Clayton Harmon are in my chapter, so I get to see them nearly every month.

We not only want to hear from the new instructors, but we check out the older ones to see whether they have learned anything since last time. I have not mentioned the incomparable LaRoy Edwards, the black-suited-and-bow-tied Willis Snyder, who is the Edison of the piano, and many others because they are still teaching another generation of technicians. I just wanted to share some color about those guys who earned those Golden Hammers and were Hall of Famers and Members of Note before some of us were born. They shared their knowledge and expertise freely to help me become a piano technician. Let us all give thanks for them and for their successors who make up PTG today.

Young Texan Meets General Lindbergh
By Fran Goodwin

Shortly after Garland and I were married, I started to work as one of two switchboard operators at Ramo-Wooldridge Corp., a small research and development company in Los Angeles. Air Force Gen. Bernard Shriever headed a division responsible for developing the nation's first intercontinental ballistic missile. Thompson Products of Cleveland was the parent company, and R-W grew by leaps and bounds. Soon there were a dozen telephone operators, and I was one of three ladies who did only long distance calls. It is easy to say I did talk to a lot very important people in the mid-50s.

Once when the Board of Directors met at the plant I helped General Charles Lindbergh with a good number of overseas telephone calls. Shortly before going home time, he came to the switchboard room to meet the young lady who had helped him. He especially liked my soft southern accent. This was a 19-year-old who had never been out of central Texas. There I was talking to a gentleman who everyone around the world knew. After shaking hands with him, I didn't want to wash my hands ever again. It is a few minutes I will never forget. It was also special to me that I got to talk with Lindbergh, who was and is a hero to Garland.

A Gift of Wings

By Garland O. Goodwin *(first published in* Logbook *magazine Dec 2003)*

Orville and Wilbur Wright gave us all a gift of wings. Like many of our kind, before and since,

Wilbur wanted to fly. What probably began as idle musing soon developed into serious contemplation of how he might soar above the earth and go wherever he wished as the birds do. He persuaded his brother to help him do that, and their quest soon claimed most of their thoughts and waking hours.

Most experimenters hoping to fly were inspired by birds. DaVinci looked at pigeons and decided that wings must flap to provide lift. Lilienthal looked at soaring birds and made a glider with a fixed wing. Newton made calculations based on deflection of air by a plane surface and satisfied himself that flight would require more power than he could imagine. The Wrights began by studying the work of others, and discovered by practical experiments that much of what was "known" was not correct.

Their success came from recognizing and solving all of the problems of lift, control and propulsion one at a time. Their predecessors risked their lives in machines that addressed only some of the problems. Many died when the other problems arose for which they had either no solution or an inadequate one. The Wrights did not climb aboard their gliders until they had proved both lateral and pitch control in tethered flights in the winds of Kitty Hawk.

When they began to make free glides they found that their rudders needed to be movable. Only when they could make long glides under complete control did they consider adding propulsion. Then they had to invent the propeller and refine internal-combustion engine design! That their "flying machine" flew the first time they tried it was the expected result of this step-by-step process of solving one problem at a time before proceeding further. So sure were they of success that they set up a camera and assigned a man to trip the shutter when their machine became airborne.

Orville won the toss and made the first short flight. Their pitch control was much too sensitive and made level flight difficult. They made four flights on December 17, 1903, the last a long one by Wilbur. He had done what he wanted to do: fly above the earth and go where he wished.

Airplane design and the art of flying them has come a long way in these hundred years, but the Wrights had the fundamentals well in hand that day at Kitty Hawk. Everything that has been done since is refinement, not invention, hundreds of patents notwithstanding. Some of the "refiners" who have made great contributions to the art and science of aeronautics might want to argue that point, but as both pilot and airplane designer, I stand by that statement, and would happily debate any challengers.

What of this wonderful gift of wings for everyone? Some of us love airplanes just for themselves because they fly and are therefore beautiful. We like to play with them, using them to chase clouds or draw figures in the sky. Others like the freedom to go in any direction without regard to rivers, hills or roads. Man-made boundaries are invisible from the air; we see just one big, wide beautiful world, all of a piece. Airplanes haul stuff and bring people together.

Some airplanes are used to tear people and things apart. That is not the airplane's fault; the bomber is as beautiful as the airliner. I wish the museums would celebrate the airplane itself as a thing of beauty and leave the politics out of it. We know what it did, and can only guess what might have happened to us if we had not had the airplane to do what it did.

Thank you, Orville and Wilbur, for making your dream and ours come true.

For Love of Airplanes
By Garland O. Goodwin *(previously unpublished)*

If you love airplanes and flying them, you will enjoy reading this. My love started early, for there were toy airplanes among my toy cars, trucks and tractors. We visited small flying fields on our Sunday drives so I absorbed the sounds and smells of the airplanes of the 30s. Those planes had tailskids, and I learned to turn my back when one approached the fence to park. The engine would roar, the flippers would go full down to raise the skid off the ground, and full rudder would swing the tail around toward us. We were showered with grass clippings and dust, but that was OK because it made me a participant!

When I was about eight years old, an airplane appeared over and near our house several times each afternoon. It had two wings, one stacked above the other, and it flew so low that I could see the people's heads in the open cockpits. I kept asking to go and see it, and the next Sunday we followed the plane to a large field where it landed. This time my father talked to the pilot, and soon we were strapped into the front seat and the plane was gathering speed across the field. I shall always remember the feeling of exhilaration that came over me when the wheels stopped bumping and the ground began to drop away from us. We sailed over the trees at the edge of the field and then high over our little town. I did not mind the loud, smelly exhaust, the fierce wind churned up by the propeller, or that the plane leaned way over when we turned. I was hooked.

I plied my dad with questions long afterward. He had to explain to me about the ailerons and how all the controls worked. I made a cardboard model and "flew" it around the house, bending the ailerons and elevators up or down as required for my maneuvers. I also liked to hold a toy airplane out the window of the car to watch the propellers spin and feel it lift when I tilted it up slightly.

When I was 16, I used earnings from my summer job at the lumber mill to take flying lessons. I had to ride the bus 20 miles to Hendersonville, and I arrived before anyone else did. I would climb into an airplane on the flight line and move the stick and rudder pedals as required by my flight of fancy. I even enjoyed the faint aroma of gasoline and the dope used to tighten the fabric.

Soon Oscar Meyer (the wiener guy is Mayer) would arrive and I would help him roll the big hangar doors open and unlock the gas pump. Oscar was a pioneer aviator who as a teenager built a glider and then an airplane and taught himself to fly. I am therefore quite pleased to have his signature in my logbook. For me it is like having a pilot license signed by Orville Wright!

Oscar had several brand new Aeronca 7AC *Champions* that he bought when the WWII GI-bill money started coming in. Unlike the Piper J3 *Cub*, the *Champ* could be flown solo in the front seat, but Oscar still put his students in the back until after primary solo.

Teaching me to fly airplanes was no easy task. I had read and studied and listened so much that I knew how to do everything already—I just needed an airplane to do it in! Ha! My air work went fairly well, straight and level and those first turns were not too wobbly (my opinion.) Of course, I could not keep the bank angle or the rate of turn constant, or the nose on the horizon. I did learn to pick a point under the left wing *before* I started a requested 90-degree turn, though.

The first sign of progress was when I flew into my propwash on completing a 360 turn. Felt pretty good about that. When we got to steep turns, it was great fun to run the nose along the horizon, while looking in the upper corner of the windshield for the rollout point. Stalls, power on and power off, were great fun, too . . . trying to keep the wings level with tender use of the rudder through the stall and subsequent recovery.

The real trouble began when I was allowed to make my first takeoff. Line up with a tree at the far end of the field, open the throttle smoothly but not too fast, stick a bit forward to raise the tail, and keep that tree centered in the windshield. Almost before I realized it, the tree was over in the right corner, and I got on the rudder. Then the tree swooshed over to the other side, but I was then on the other pedal. Then I could feel Oscar overriding my efforts and things settled down as we became airborne. Whew! This ain't as easy as I expected!

Gentle turns in the climb, and we stay in the pattern to come on around and land. Oscar half-turned in his seat to explain landing technique again, illustrating with his hand on top of the instrument panel. Having practiced slow fight and climbing and gliding turns, I flew a pretty decent traffic pattern, turning base and final when Oscar suggested. I lined up with the runway, and continued the glide, skirting a little hill on our right, and beginning the flare too soon. Oscar added power when I failed to do so in time, and with the whole situation going rapidly from bad to worse, he opened the throttle and signaled a go-around.

Soon we were spending half of my hour on air work and the other half doing "circuits and bumps." In the air I practiced rectangular course and S-turns across a road, and learned how to enter spins all sorts of ways and recover from them after exactly three turns. I was amazed to learn that full aileron applied at stall would cause the *Champ* to fall into a spin in the opposite direction! I was really beginning to enjoy my newfound skills.

After a while I learned how to plan an approach to touch down where I wanted to, and I enjoyed listening to everything unwind as I held it off as long as possible, working the stick all the way back. The idea was to have the wheels roll onto the ground just as the wing stalled: a perfect "three-point" landing. But the rollout was something else; soon we were zig-zagging all over the place.

Oscar sent me up with other instructors from time to time. Tommy Stocks had gone through school with Oscar and then flew C-46s over the "Hump" during WWII. Tommy was a friendly, easy-going guy with a ready grin who also could make an airplane do his bidding perfectly. We did chandelles and lazy-eights to further hone my skills in the air, but the landings were always the same.

As long as I was in the air, the rudder pedals posed no problem, but on the ground, I would get on the wrong one as often as not. Why? When I was a small boy my cousin built me a "soap box" car with a front axle pivoted on a bolt for steering. We steered with our feet on the front axle bar; to go right we pushed with our left foot and vice versa. Perfectly natural, right?

When the controls of airplanes were finally standardized, they had a pivoted bar to operate the rudder. That was also considered natural, because the adverse yaw created by aileron deflection required a coordinated use of the rudder to produce a pure roll. Left rudder with left stick. That was fine for rolling into turns, but backward for steering on the ground. So I had some unlearning to do!

When my rollouts finally became confined to the middle of the runway area, Tommy began to subtly induce turns to be sure I would respond quickly and correctly on the rudder pedals. After a few pretty bad landings one sunny day (I did manage to get and keep the Champ on the runway) Tommy got on the brakes in the runup area and announced that he was going to "get out of this airplane before you kill me!" Then he flashed that boyish grin and told me to make three full-stop landings and call it a day.

Without Tommy on board the little *Champ* fairly leapt into the air. Rolling out on downwind it finally hit me that I was really up in this airplane by myself and I would therefore have to make this landing by myself. I extended the downwind leg a little bit because I thought the *Champ* might glide flatter, and gave the little hill a wide berth so I had to turn slightly to line up on final. The slight breeze was right down the middle, and I was a little high. I held the approach speed though, and when I flared it settled in OK. A tiny bounce, but I held it straight on the rollout.

Oscar did not allow running takeoffs until after solo, so it was a long ride back to the other end of the runway. I remembered to taxi slowly and do my S-turns, but I really wanted to get back into the air! The second landing was just about perfect, and the third was OK, and when I taxied to the gas pump I tried to look casual as I was the only one to get out of the airplane.

When I walked into the office, they grabbed me and cut off part of my shirttail. I got to write my name on it and they tacked it up on the bulletin board with the others. Of course I still had a LOT to learn about flying airplanes, but it was good to be on that first rung of the tall ladder leading to a pilot's license. Both my job and the money to fly ended when school started, but I had something then that no one could ever take away from me: I had flown a real airplane all by myself!

Tommy bought a surplus Stearman that summer, and I laid out the numbers on the rudder with masking tape for him. I had hoped thereby to get a ride in it, but he bought me a hamburger and fries instead. When the big Stinson went out on a passenger hop, Tommy told me to take the right seat, so I did get a free airplane ride. Tommy paid $850 for his Stearman, and many "airport bums" told him he was crazy because they were available at such-and-such for only $300. Tommy's Stearman had 12 hours total time on engine and airframe when he arrived at Oscar's flying field.

I continued my flight training at Pikes Airport in San Diego some ten years later. Pikes was two hangars and a portion of the sands of Mission Bay. The five towers of the low frequency range station claimed a lot of the airspace partially enclosed by the downwind, base, and final approach legs for "runway" 27. This runway was defined somewhat by a few light fixtures scattered along its length. The takeoffs in dry sand took a bit longer, but the sand was very forgiving on landings.

Here I found some vintage Champs and two female flight instructors, one of whom had an Airline Transport Rating. Her name was Carolyn, but she went by "Mac." For my first dual they sent me out with Jeannie, who looked at my logbook, put me in the front seat, and said let's go. There was really nothing to see across the bay, but I started a takeoff run anyway. By the time the tail came up, Jeannie was screaming for me to get off the pedals—she could not overpower me to straighten us out!

So it was back to square one. Soon Norm took me out to the practice area and really taught me how to fly. He liked nothing better than to get me really involved in some training exercise, only to suddenly chop the throttle and shout with great glee, "forced landing!" Of course we were usually at about 400 feet AGL with a high tension power line between us and the only barely suitable landing spot in the area.

For my *second* primary solo, I had to buy a case of "Oly" (Olympia beer from Washington state). That was also the penalty for taxiing in with the flaps down, or leaving the master switch on after shutting down the Cessna 172.

Mac was the instrument and multi-engine instructor, and there was no instrument requirement in those days for a private ticket. However, Mac and I had to go up in the "instrument" ship, a Cessna 140 with a full gyro panel and radios, so I could learn to do "fade 90s." That was a procedure for determining your location by tuning in a range station and crossing one of its "beams," then making a 90-degree turn. By listening to the signal fade there was a way to figure out where you were in relation to the range station. I don't remember any more about it, probably because I had no enthusiasm for it.

When it was time to learn night landings, it was Norm who volunteered to come back after supper and show me the ropes. There were only three runway lights working and there was a light on the limp windsock. I got off okay, and he told me to climb to 4,000 feet over the middle of the bay. It was a beautiful starry night, and the lights of civilization were far away. When I completed the climb, Norm said to put my head down between my knees and close my eyes until he told me to look up.

I did, and I felt the airplane rolling and turning, pulling positive and negative Gs, the engine howling sometimes in protest. Finally things quieted down a bit, and Norm yelled "You got it!" I grabbed the stick, put my feet on the pedals and began to look around for something—anything! There was only black with a few twinkling stars ahead, and off one wing there was a string of city lights running perpendicular to the bottom surface of the wing behind the trailing edge. We were climbing straight up! I rammed both the stick and the throttle to the firewall and we were soon in a level attitude, but with no airspeed indicated and the ship getting a little wobbly. Norm is laughing his head off back there! When the speed picked up, we were straight and level at 3000 feet.

Seeing no lights moving in any of our airspace, he told me to cut the throttle and lay it over in a 60-

degree banked turn and hold it until we got down to a thousand feet. That was fun. Then we headed for the red lights of the range station towers and turned base, and I then lined up between two runway lights on the left and one on the right for final approach. Norm said that I should flare high, add a little power and hold a three-point attitude until touchdown. The Champ settled into the soft sand without a whimper.

We had stuck a landing light into a socket near the wingtip, and made sure our navigation lights were all on, before we took off. However, we only turned the landing light on briefly while taxiing in so as not to overheat it. We had landed in the blackest hole I ever saw, and I kept it straight by a few lights visible on the other side of the bay. After a few more landings Norm signed me off for night flight.

Soon it was time for the check ride for my private license. Since my uncorrected vision had deteriorated to well below the minimum requirement, I had to be checked by the regional FAA Inspector, a retired Marine Corps Colonel. I picked him up at Lindbergh Field and off we went. I had a pretty bad case of "Inspectoritis" and really blew the ride. I am ashamed of that cryptic entry in my logbook, "Private ride NG" and his signature.

The crusty Colonel suggested that I get five more hours of dual before I came back to try again. I then flew with ALL of the instructors in turn, as they each put me back through the wringer in their own way.

Since this was to be a "medical flight test," I had to do very well on it in order to get a waiver of the uncorrected vision requirement. Mac decided that I should do a circuit of the field without my glasses, even though I would be required to carry an extra pair in the plane at all times.

I told her I felt OK about it, but she would have to watch for other airplanes. She was used to that chore since she usually had her charges under the hood. I gave her a nice straight takeoff, flew a nearly perfect traffic pattern (I had to lean close to read the altimeter to fly downwind at exactly 600 feet), and then used my night landing technique for a soft touchdown. Mac was so pleased she told everybody about me!

When I went back, the Inspector greeted me warmly and put me at ease right away. I then proceeded to give him an exemplary ride: all the maneuvers right by the book, and I even approached my forced landing spot *into the wind.*

With my new ticket, I got checked out in all the rental airplanes on the field and gave rides to all my friends. It was Mac who had the wisdom to show me how to fly passengers, especially first timers: she said that I should never move the flight controls far enough for the passenger to see them move, and had me demonstrate. By golly, it is possible! The flying school owners got involved in aircraft financing, and they let me ferry airplanes to build time and gain experience. Then four of us went together and bought a Taylorcraft BC-12D.

In the meantime I had been sent by my company to test ejectors for the new F-106 at Daingerfield, near Longview TX. There I met Bill Reed, who invited me to fly with him on fire patrol for the US Forest Service on Saturday morning. I was waiting for Bill at the appointed airstrip when he arrived in a 150-horse Super Cub. I climbed in the back, and as soon as I was buckled in, Bill made a forward motion and said "Let's go . . . and try to hold 'er down to 90 in the climb." [90 is about all a *Champ* will do wide open.]

The Cub leapt forward when I opened the throttle, and was airborne almost immediately from the three-point attitude. I had to really pull the nose up to keep the airspeed down to 90. The day looked like rain was imminent, and the radio soon told us to abort the patrol. Bill "Rogered" and then told me we would make the beer run over to the adjacent wet county. We landed in an open field and parked next to a fence across from a little country store.

After securing several cases in the baggage compartment, Bill put me in front for the return trip. When I told him I had not learned how to do loops, he just hauled the Cub up and over, adding power on the way up and pulling it off as we started down the back side. Then he told me how to do it, and I did several. Since there were clouds that day I had some references to keep it in a vertical plane, and I hit my propwash each time after the first one.

Later Bill flew a Cessna 180 for a missionary group in Africa, and his adventures appeared in the AOPA *Pilot* magazine. Meanwhile, I went back to try some loops in our Taylorcraft: nose down a little to pick up maneuvering speed, add full throttle as the nose comes up with the yoke full back into my chest, watch for the inverted horizon in the top of the windshield, reduce power to idle going back down, bring power back up to cruise at level flight. The T-craft looped so tightly that I was higher than when I started, so did not hit my prop wash. I soon learned how much of everything was required to do a fairly round loop and hit my propwash and entry altitude.

When we moved to Texas we bought into a Luscombe 8A *Silvaire*. It soon became apparent that if I were going to fly in the winds of Texas, I would have to learn to make wheel landings. Sid rode along to show and tell, and it wasn't long until a fellow pilot said "I saw you painting them on out there" when I walked in from tying the bird down. All pilots watch other pilots land, but nothing is said unless the landings are very good.

Sid decided to put on an air fair to drum up business for his flying field. We had bomb drops from 200 feet AGL (small paper bags of sand), spot landings (you cannot add power at any time after turning final), and balloon busting. I took along a young neighbor boy as my bombardier, and we were intrigued to see that the scoring guys were leaning on the target barrel as we came over for the drop; they had found that to be the safest place around!

I did not win the spot landing contest, and the balloon deal was probably the most fun. My wife accompanied me for this, and they gave us TWO huge balloons inflated with air, not helium, so they began to fall slowly as soon as they were "released." If you have ever been in a Luscombe, you know that there is barely room for two normal sized adults. Fran had to push the door open far enough to get a balloon out without popping it. We put them out at 3000 feet and had to break off the "attack" at 1500 feet.

Now you would think that with a five-foot propeller spinning out front that you could not miss. First off, I did not wait long enough after release to turn back. I found the thing OK, bobbing just below the horizon, but it was in the top of my windshield and I had to tighten up the turn as I closed on it. I thought I had hit it since it whooshed right in, centered in the windshield. I continued to turn to get back over the airport, and there was that balloon, seeming to grin at me defiantly.

On my next pass, I had to go to a vertical bank and pull the stick all the way back just to get close. Then I felt the first nibble of the coming stall, and of course I dumped the stick and rammed in full throttle to avoid the spin. I never did get to bust a balloon, since I ran out of ideas and altitude both times. In watching others attempt it, I saw the balloon just simply go above or below the airplane instead of through the prop. At subsonic speeds, an airplane does part the air a good ways in front of it, and the balloon just went where the air did.

I was determined to master landing in crosswinds with gusts, so I would stop by the airport on my way home from work, remove the tiedown chain, and see whether the wind would try to lift the wing away from me. If it did not, I would just re-attach the chain and go on home. On most windy days, I was the only fool flying an airplane off that field.

One day the wind picked up while I was doing my circuits, and I found that I could not track the runway centerline unless the upwind wing was down too much to land. What to do? Any sensible person would have gone over to another field with a runway better aligned with the wind. But this fool continued the approach, and then turned 45 degrees toward the wind, and rolled the left wheel onto the taxiway with the wingtip maybe two feet off the pavement. I continued this way until I could turn right in a wide sweeping turn to roll into my tiedown space. As the turn progressed, I brought the wing up to let the right wheel start rolling. I let the tail down as the speed bled off, then full down elevator when the wind came from behind. I braked to a stop in my space, tied the bird down, and headed for my car.

The retired USAF Master Sergeant who ran the airport came out of the office shack to yell at me. "Dammit, Goodwin, you keep that up and one day you are going to roll that airplane up into a ball, and I am gonna have to try to pry what's left of you out of it!"

All of that practice did pay off for me. I had my whole family in a Piper PA-20 *Pacer* headed for Texas. We had been weathered in at Atlanta for a couple of days, and the big HIGH that rose over Texas to clear it out gave us a stiff headwind. When we finally arrived over our intended refueling stop, I saw that it had only one runway, 18-36. I then checked the map, and the next airport on our course had long runways like the letter K. So we chugged on over there, only to find big white Xs on the other runways. With only 18-36 available, and gas now low, it had to be runway 36 instead of the hoped-for 32.

Good thing the *Pacer* has stubby wings! I came down final with the left wing down about 20 degrees and Fran's bowed head in her hands. She could not look. The Lord was surely with me as I leveled out and rolled that left wheel on so gently that when Fran finally looked up we were rolling slowly toward the gas pump area. She had not realized that we had landed!

On the way again, we could see the great Mississippi River on the horizon, but it seemed to stay there. With that 30-knot headwind, the westbound cars below were almost keeping up with us! Then the airplane began to slow slightly, then speed up again. I checked all the instruments, but all of them were OK. Then I turned around to check the kids (aged about 5 and 7), and found that they were leaning forward. Then they hurled themselves mightily against the seat back. That action slowed the plane just enough to be noticeable.

Returning from another trip in a *Pacer*, again with the whole family aboard, I decided to let down though the scattered clouds before they got closer together. As we rocked a little between clouds the engine began to miss. Better put on the carb heat; that's better. With the field in sight on the horizon, the engine began to run less and stop more. Guess it must have iced up after all . . . then it quit altogether. At 2000 feet AGL in a *Pacer* with no power, you are going to land right here, not somewhere over there.

Fortunately, there are plenty of suitable fields in central Texas, and I lined up into the wind and set 'er down softly in the grass. On the rollout, a big light bulb went on in my noggin. I had not switched tanks because Fran and the kids were asleep and I didn't want to startle her; well, they were jolly well wide awake now! The kids were admiring several cows who looked up to see what we were. I switched to the full tank in the other wing, hit the starter, taxied back to the fence, and took off for the short hop over to the airport. I don't know what all I was supposed to learn that day, but I always switched tanks at the first sputter after that. And I was pleased that I had made a successful forced landing.

There is a lot more to tell, but I hope my fellow pilots have found many parallels with their own experience in this small offering. And I hope the wannabes still wannabe. Airplanes are wonderful toys, but we have to treat them nice or they will bite. I hope your only bite is from the flying bug. Happy landings!

Pilot in Command

By Garland O. Goodwin *(Previously unpublished, but has been given three times as a talk before pilot groups. It is offered as given, with no explanation of terms that pilots will understand.)*

As both aeronautical engineer and private pilot, I was a bit of an oddity in the airplane design groups of the big companies I worked for. Most of the people designing the airplanes were not pilots and were interested only in building an airplane that would meet its performance specs and not come apart doing what it was designed to do.

I was proud to enter time in my logbook as "pilot in command." It meant that I was in the left seat and responsible for getting the bird off the ground and back down again in a condition that would allow it to be flown again—immediately. I took that responsibility seriously, and when I was an active pilot I practiced my pilot skills continually.

As a designer of airplanes, I took seriously the idea that the guy in the left seat must be "in command" of his airplane at all times. He must not become just another passenger in an airplane that is suddenly doing its own thing. In any discussions of design considerations I always took the pilot's side and viewpoint, and upon meeting opposition, I tended to get loud and insistent. Probably why I never became a chief engineer.

I was a new hire of less than a year when I discovered that one of the five wing designs proposed for Convair's new jetliner (the 880) would drag the outboard engine pylon if landed when banked only 5 degrees. We land small airplanes in crosswinds that require more bank than that to keep them lined up on approach, so I asked some of the ex-military pilot engineers who had flown heavies about it. They got rid of that wing before it hatched.

With sharply swept wings, the roll-yaw coupling resulting in "Dutch roll" can be practically eliminated by drooping the wings. Designers of military cargo airplanes like the C-5 and its successors put the wing on top, let it droop, and thus get the fuselage close to the ground for loading things like tanks. However, the FAA decreed that airline jets would have low wings with the engines below them so that any turbine blades that decided to part company from the engine would be absorbed by the wing rather than the passenger cabin. The aero guy who proposed that 880 wing was just trying to please everybody.

About this time a German company offered a smaller jet with the engines mounted on the fuselage near the tail. Good design from transonic drag standpoint, but FAA was adamant: no fuel lines in the fuselage! But politics prevailed: in order to sell our airplanes over there, we have to let them sell theirs over here.

With the dam breached, we were soon deluged with the DC-9 and 10, the Lockheed 1011, and even Boeing brought out the hot-rod 727. Of course I was agin' it, but I had no part in any of those designs. The TBO for the center engines on 727s and 1011s was a lot less than the side-mounted ones because of the bad airflow in the S-duct. Douglas avoided that on the DC-10, but I was uneasy about having that potential buzz-saw mounted where it could cut all the connections between the cockpit and the tail feathers.

Everyone now remembers what followed when it did finally happen. The flight crew became passengers like everybody else. But they did some good head scratching and remembered that the throttles affect the trim of an airplane, and they actually brought it successfully to the threshold of a runway! But my thought is that if they had not put engines near the tail that would not have happened, and more than a hundred people might still be alive today.

I always thought that the stick and rudder pedals should be connected mechanically to the control surfaces they are supposed to move. The power assist should be an add-on, like the power steering on your car. It started on military airplanes, but fully powered flight controls with artificial feel soon became the norm.

The Vought F8U Crusader is a good example. It was in production when I arrived at Vought in 1961, but I did get to put the "direct lift flap" mod on it for

the French Navy. Anyway, the engineers put the hydraulic pumps near the middle, nestled in primary structure to save weight of armor plate to protect them. If the bird took a hit there, it was going down anyway and would not need the pumps any more.

Nevertheless, an F8U pilot lost his hydraulics over the Nam and soon found himself a passenger in a bird that did not respond to any control inputs, including the throttle. As he contemplated pulling the curtain to eject, the bird pulled out of its dive and began to climb again. When it topped out and started down again, he could see his carrier, so he decided to stay aboard for a while and see what would happen next. Each time it completed the large loop he was closer to the ship, so he waited until he was over water to eject. He was picked up to fly another day.

This event caused the Navy to ask for fully connected mechanical linkages in the A7. Even if you lost the hydraulics you could still steer the bird home and perhaps land it. Score one for our side.

Next I got to work on the great Boeing 747. I was still a Vought employee, and when we arrived in Seattle, the Boeing people were obviously delighted to have lost the C-5 design competition. With most of the development cost paid by Uncle Sam, they could now build the commercial airliner they wanted. We got the information we needed and went back to Dallas to design and build the aft fuselage and tail feathers.

I was assigned to the vertical tail, but we had meetings so that all of our stuff would "look like it came out of the same shop." The normally fixed horizontal stabilizer was to be pivoted for trim by a jackscrew powered by an electric motor. Even with the recirculating ball bearings, a jackscrew cannot be driven by its load. So if the jackscrew motor ran away and went to the end of its travel and stopped for good, the stabilizer would be stuck there for good, too.

Having owned an airplane whose trim mechanism often liked to stay where it was and not respond to the crank in the cockpit, I began to ask questions. Will the elevators be big enough to overcome an undesired position of the stabilizer? Answer was a big and impatient "NO!" Jackscrews are very reliable etc. etc.; the bosses did not want to hear any more about it. Fast forward about thirty years, and how many airplanes (NOT 747s) were lost or nearly so when improperly lubricated jackscrews misbehaved?

There is a big difference between military airplanes and commercial airplanes. I am more tolerant of new-fangled ideas on military planes, because the crew can punch out if things go bad. I will even admit that the autopilot or the computer can fly an airplane straight and level, or to a destination, better than I can. I get bored doing straight and level! The military is welcome to their fighters that are so unstable that they MUST be flown by computer. What disturbs me is that when I retired, the designers of the next generation of commercial airliners were looking at tail surfaces so small they could function only as trim surfaces (less drag and less weight.)

When I learned my trade, we worked hard on the aerodynamics to make airplanes behave as the pilots were trained to expect. If you wanted to pull more Gs you had to pull back harder on the stick. The wing was designed to create turbulence on the tail to warn you that it was approaching a stall. The wing root would stall first, further increasing the turbulence that you would feel in the stick tied to the elevators. And the outer part of the wing would still be flying so that you would have some aileron control. So if you want to stall the wing, you have to work at it: more and more up elevator to keep the angle of attack increasing because the wing is designed to create an ever-increasing nose down pitching moment as its angle of attack increases.

Another of those five wings for the Convair 880 was discovered in the wind tunnel to change to a nose up pitching moment as angle of attack increased. It also was promptly thrown out. This is the American way.

The Germans, on the other hand, like to design their airplanes with wings and balanced control surfaces such that the entire flight envelope of maneuvers could be performed with only a fingertip on top of the stick. Therefore the airplanes have no "feel" as we American pilots understand it. That is the way the new commercial airliners will be designed, since computers will control them, and the hydraulic cylinders moving the surfaces can therefore be very small as well. But it is hard for me to believe that some hapless pilot is not going to find himself low and slow some day and need bigger tail feathers to get something good to happen.

Nowadays the pilot "flies" the computer and the computer flies the airplane. This is called "fly-by-wire." I cannot forget the film of the new Airbus continuing right into the ground as the pilot tried frantically to make a go-around. He had the throttle levers full forward, was trying to raise the flaps, and was hauling back on the yoke. But he had neglected to tell the computer that he wanted to climb, so it continued the descent. Who was in command that day?

How many of you have flown the great North American T6? Did you know that it has servo-tabs on the ailerons to reduce the load at the stick as the deflection angle increases? Enables you to get a fast roll rate without working up a sweat. Did you also know that those little tabs can be maladjusted so that they can drive the aileron to full travel after a small initial deflection? That would sure get your attention, wouldn't it? Are you beginning to appreciate that the designers and maintainers have to do a good job in order for you to be able to do your job well, too? Makes us all happy when we get it right . . .

Made in the USA
Charleston, SC
22 December 2009